African Americans

IN MINNESOTA

David Vassar Taylor

Foreword by Bill Holm

MINNESOTA HISTORICAL SOCIETY PRESS

Cover: Jack, Bob, and Ralph Jones in front of 369 Jay (Galtier) St., St. Paul, in 1929

Publication of this book was supported, in part, with funds provided by the June D. Holmquist Publication Endowment Fund of the Minnesota Historical Society.

www.mnhs.org/mhspress

Manufactured in Canada

10 9 8 7 6 5 4 3 2 1

International Standard Book Number: 0-87351-420-3

⊗ The paper used in this publication meets the minimum requirements of the American National Standard for Information Sciences Permanence for Printed Library Materials, ANSI Z 39.48-1984.

Library of Congress Cataloging-in-Publication Data

Taylor, David Vassar, 1945–
   African Americans in Minnesota / David Vassar Taylor ; foreword by Bill Holm.
     p.   cm. — (The people of Minnesota)
   Includes bibliographical references and index.
   ISBN 0-87351-420-3 (alk. paper)
     1. African Americans—Minnesota—History. 2. African Americans—Minnesota—Social conditions. 3. Minnesota—History. 4. Minnesota—Ethnic relations. I. Title. II. Series.

F615.N4 T39 2002
977.6'00496073—dc21

2002005812

This book was designed and set in type by Wendy Holdman, Stanton Publication Services, St. Paul, Minnesota; it was printed by Friesens, Altona, Manitoba.

Contents

Foreword

by Bill Holm

Human beings have not been clever students at learning any lessons from their three or four thousand odd years of recorded history. We repeat our mistakes from generation to generation with tedious regularity. But we ought to have learned at least one simple truth: that there is no word, no idea that is not a double-edged sword. Take, for example, the adjective *ethnic.* In one direction, it cuts upward, to show us the faces, the lives, the histories of our neighbors and ourselves. It shows us that we are not alone on this planet—that we are all rooted with deep tendrils growing down to our ancestors and the stories of how they came to be not *there,* but *here.* These tendrils are visible in our noses and cheekbones, our middle-aged diseases and discomforts, our food, our religious habits, our celebrations, our manner of grieving, our very names. The fact that here in Minnesota, at any rate, we mostly live together in civil harmony—showing sometimes affectionate curiosity, sometimes puzzled irritation but seldom murderous violence—speaks well for our progress as a community of neighbors, even as members of a civilized human tribe.

But early in this new century in America we have seen the dark blade of the ethnic sword made visible, and it has cut us to the quick. From at least one angle, our national wounds from terrorist attacks are an example of ethnicity gone mad, tribal loyalty whipped to fanatical hysteria, until it turns human beings into monstrous machines of mass murder. Few tribes own a guiltless history in this regard.

The 20th century did not see much progress toward solving the problem of ethnicity. Think of Turk and Armenian, German and Jew, Hutu and Tutsi, Protestant and Catholic, Albanian and Serb, French and Algerian—think of our own lynchings. We all hoped for better from the 21st century but may not get any reprieve at all from the tidal waves of violence and hatred.

As global capitalism breaks down the borders between nation-states, fanatical ethnicity rises to life like a hydra. Cheerful advertisements assure us that we are all a family—wearing the same pants, drinking the same pop, singing and going on line together as we spend. When we invoke *family,* we don't seen to remember well the ancient Greek family tragedies. We need to make not a family but a civil community of neighbors, who may neither spend nor look alike but share a desire for truthful history—an alert curiosity about the stories and the lives of our neighbors and a respect both for difference—and for privacy. We must get the metaphors right; we are neither brothers nor sisters here in Minnesota, nor even cousins. We are neighbors, all us *ethnics,* and that fact imposes on us a stricter obligation than blood and, to the degree to which we live up to it, makes us civilized.

As both Minnesotans and Americans, none of us can escape the fact that we *ethnics,* in historic terms, have hardly settled here for the length of a sneeze. Most of us have barely had time to lose the language of our ancestors or to produce protein-stuffed children half a foot taller than ourselves. What does a mere century or a little better amount to in history? Even the oldest settlers—the almost ur-inhabitants, the Dakota and Ojibwa—emigrated here from elsewhere on the continent. The Jeffers Petroglyphs in southwest Minnesota are probably the oldest evidence we have of any human habitation. They are still and will most likely remain only shadowy tellers of any historic truth about us. Who made this language? History is silent. The only clear facts scholars agree on about these mysterious pictures carved in hard red Sioux quartzite is that they were the work of neither of the current native tribes and can be scientifically dated only between the melting of the last glacier and the arrival of the first European settlers in the territory. They seem very old to the eye. It is good for us, I think, that our history begins not with certainty, but with mystery, cause for wonder rather than warfare.

In 1978, before the first edition of this ethnic survey appeared, a researcher came to Minneota to interview local people for information about the Icelanders. Tiny though their numbers, the Icelanders were a real ethnic group with their own language, history, and habits of mind. They settled in the late 19th century in three small clumps around Minneota. At that time, I could still introduce this researcher to a few old ladies born in Iceland and to a dozen children of immigrants who grew up with English as a second language, thus with thick accents. The old still prayed the Lord's Prayer in Icelandic, to them the language of Jesus himself, and a handful of people could still read the ancient poems and sagas in the leather-covered editions brought as treasures from the old country. But two decades have wiped out that primary source. The first generation is gone, only a few alert and alive in the second, and the third speaks only English—real Americans in hardly a century. What driblets of Icelandic blood remain are mixed with a little of this, a little of that. The old thorny names, so difficult to pronounce, have been respelled, then corrected for sound.

Is this the end of ethnicity? The complete meltdown into history evaporated into global marketing anonymity? I say no. On a late October day, a letter arrives from a housewife in Nevis, Minnesota. She's never met me, but she's been to Iceland now and met unknown cousins she found on an Internet genealogy search. The didactic voice in my books reminds her of her father's voice: "He could've said that. Are we *all* literary?" We've never met, she confesses, but she gives me enough of her family tree to convince me that we might be cousins fifteen generations back. She is descended, she says with pride, from the Icelandic law speaker in 1063, Gunnar the Wise. She knows now that she is not alone in history. She has shadowing names, even dates, in her very cells. She says—with more smug pride—that her vinarterta (an Icelandic immigrant prune cake that is often the last surviving ghost of the old country) is better than any she ate in Iceland. She invites me to sample a piece if I ever get to Nevis. Who says there is no profit and joy in ethnicity? That killjoy has obviously never tasted vinarterta!

I think what is happening in this letter, both psychologically and culturally, happens simultaneously in the lives of hundreds of thousands of Minnesotans and countless millions of Americans. Only the details differ, pilaf, jiaozi, fry bread, collards, latkes, or menudo rather than vinarterta, but the process and the object remain the same. We came to this cold flat place so far from the sea in wave after wave of immigration—filling up the steadily fewer empty places in this vast midsection of a continent—but for all of us, whatever the reason for our arrival: poverty, political upheaval, ambition—we check most of our history, and thus our inner life, at the door of the new world. For a while, old habits and even the language carry on, but by the third generation, history is lost. Yet America's history, much less Minnesota's, is so tiny, so new, so uncertain, so much composed of broken connections—and now of vapid media marketing—that we feel a loneliness for a history that stretches back further into the life of the planet. We want more cousins so that, in the best sense, we can be better neighbors. We can acquire interior weight that will keep us rooted in our new homes. That is why we need to read these essays on the ethnic history of Minnesota. We need to meet those neighbors and listen to new stories.

We need also the concrete underpinning of facts that they provide to give real body to our tribal myths if those myths are not to drift off into nostalgic vapor. Svenskarnas Dag and Santa Lucia Day will not tell us much about the old Sweden that disgorged so many of its poor to Minnesota. At the height of the Vietnam War, an old schoolmate of mine steeled his courage to confess to his stern Swedish father that he was thinking both of conscientious objection and, if that didn't work, escape to Canada. He expected patriotic disdain, even contempt. Instead the upright old man wept and cried, "So soon again!" He had left Sweden early in the century to avoid the compulsory military draft but told that history to none of his children. The history of our arrival here does not lose its nobility by being filled with draft-dodging, tubercular lungs, head lice, poverty, failure. It gains humanity. We are all members of a very big club—and not an exclusive one.

I grew up in western Minnesota surrounded by accents: Icelandic, Norwegian, Swedish, Belgian, Dutch, German, Polish, French Canadian, Irish, even a Yankee or two, a French Jewish doctor, and a Japanese chicken sexer in Dr. Kerr's chicken hatchery. As a boy, I thought that a fair-sized family of nations. Some of those tribes have declined almost to extinction, and new immigrants have come to replace them: Mexican, Somali, Hmong, and Balkan. Relations are sometimes awkward as the old ethnicities bump their aging dispositions against the new, forgetting that their own grandparents spoke English strangely, dressed in odd clothes, and ate foods that astonished and sometimes repulsed their neighbors. History does not cease moving at the exact moment we begin to occupy it comfortably.

I've taught many Laotian students in my freshman English classes at Southwest State University in Marshall. I always assign papers on family history. For many children of the fourth generation, the real stories have evaporated, but for the Hmong, they are very much alive—escape followed by gunfire, swimming the Mekong, a childhood in Thai refugee camps. One student brought a piece of his mother's intricate embroidery to class and translated its symbolic storytelling language for his classmates. Those native-born children of farmers will now be haunted for life by the dark water of the Mekong. Ethnic history is alive and surprisingly well in Minnesota.

Meanwhile the passion for connection—thus a craving for a deeper history—has blossomed grandly in my generation and the new one in front of it. A Canadian professional genealogist at work at an immigrant genealogical center at Hofsos in north Iceland assures me, as fact, that genealogy has surpassed, in raw numbers, both stamp and coin collecting as a hobby. What will it next overtake? Baseball cards? Rock and roll 45 rpms? It's a sport with a future, and these essays on ethnic history are part of the evidence of its success.

I've even bought a little house in Hofsos, thirty miles south of the Arctic Circle where in the endless summer light I watch loads of immigrant descendants from Canada and the United States arrive clutching old brown-tone photos, yellowed letters in languages they don't read, the misspelled name of Grandpa's farm. They feed their information into computers and comb through heavy books, hoping to find the history lost when their ancestors simplified their names at Ellis Island or in Quebec. To be ethnic, somehow, is to be human. Neither can we escape it, nor should we want to. You cannot interest yourself in the lives of your neighbors if you don't take sufficient interest in your own.

Minnesotans often jokingly describe their ethnic backgrounds as "mongrel"—a little of this, a little of that, who knows what? But what a gift to be a mongrel! So many ethnicities and so little time in life to track them down! You will have to read many of these essays to find out who was up to what, when. We should also note that every one of us on this planet is a mongrel, thank God. The mongrel is the strongest and longest lived of dogs—and of humans, too. Only the dead are pure—and then, only in memory, never in fact. Mongrels do not kill each other to maintain the pure ideology of the tribe. They just go on mating, acquiring a richer ethnic history with every passing generation. So I commend this series to you. Let me introduce you to your neighbors. May you find pleasure and wisdom in their company.

African Americans

IN MINNESOTA

Bill and Ralph Gardner lent a hand at clearing snow from the sidewalk in front of their house at 369-375 Jay (later Galtier) Street in St. Paul in 1912.

FOR MORE THAN 150 YEARS the twin cities of Minneapolis and St. Paul have been home to small, independent, and industrious African American communities. A survey at the end of the 20th century identified the Twin Cities as one of the pockets of black affluence in the United States. Another based on 1990 census data announced that African Americans in the Twin Cities possessed one of the highest levels of postsecondary degrees in the nation. Ten years earlier, a magazine survey of the nation's metropolitan areas declared Minneapolis was one of the best-kept secrets with regard to livability for African Americans.[1]

African Americans, also referred to as blacks, comprise the second largest racial group in the United States. According to the 2000 census, African Americans alone or in combination with one or more other races numbered 36.4 million persons or 12.9% of the national population. For purposes of the census, black or African American referred to people who have origins in any of the black race groups of Africa or Africans in diaspora and who are listed among the protected groups in the United States. This number may not include more recent immigrants from the African continent who are of black African descent. Although considered a racial group by the census, blacks can also be a cultural definition as in the case of black Hispanics.[2] In 2000 a total of 171,731 Minnesotans (3.4%) identified themselves as African American/black while an additional 31,241 claimed a mixed racial heritage.

A significant number of Minnesotans of African descent were born in Africa, naturalized, or born to immigrant parents in the United States. They are culturally and racially distinct from African Americans. They are increasingly represented in the work force, the economy, and the cultural life of the Twin Cities metropolitan area. These new Minnesotans are more geographically dispersed across

Minnesota than African Americans who have traditionally resided in more populous urban areas.³

African Americans are ethnically distinct having well-defined cultural characteristics that reflect primarily a synthesis of African and European heritages. Although in the past American society has exhibited ambivalence toward their integration into the mainstream, as a people they have contributed immeasurably to the physical expansion, economic well-being, and cultural development of the United States. Their urban communities have achieved a high degree of cohesion through well-developed institutions such as churches, newspapers, fraternal groups, social clubs, and political organizations.

African Americans are the only racial, ethnic, or national group brought involuntarily to North America as slave labor for the emerging agrarian economy. During the entire period of the Atlantic slave trade from 1510 to the 1860s, approximately 8,000,000 to 10,500,000 Africans were imported into South America, the islands of the Caribbean, and the North American continent. It has been estimated that at least 348,000 slaves were brought from the west coast of Africa to British North America from 1619 to 1808. Their importation into the United States was legally prohibited in 1808, but another 51,000 are thought to have been smuggled into the southern states between 1808 and the outbreak of the Civil War. In 1861 the United States had about 4,000,000 black Americans. In the years following the Civil War, many of them migrated from the South in search of greater economic opportunities and political freedom. In the succeeding century, such migrations ebbed and flowed to industrial cities of the Northeast, Midwest, and West.⁴

Early Settlement

The earliest records of persons of African descent in what is now Minnesota date from the closing years of the 18th century when the British still effectively controlled the fur trade of the region. The best known of the fur traders of African descent were Pierre Bonga (or Bungo) and his son George, who was born near the site of Duluth about 1802. George married an Ojibwe woman. More than 100 of their descendants lived in the Leech Lake region as late as 1900. Bungo Township and Bungo Brook in Cass County and Lake Bonga on the White Earth Reservation were named for this pioneer family.[5]

Fur trader George Bonga sat for St. Paul photographer C. A. Zimmerman in 1870. His formal attire included moccasins, which call attention to his connections to northern Minnesota's Ojibwe communities.

The next group of people of African descent to reach Minnesota were slaves owned by officers stationed at Fort Snelling and by southern families who vacationed in Minnesota during the summer months. History has accorded varying degrees of attention to five persons—Rachael, a slave who spent the years 1831–34 at various army posts in Minnesota and Wisconsin and sued for her freedom before the Missouri Supreme Court in 1835; Dred Scott and his wife, Harriet Robinson Scott, whose two-year residence at Fort Snelling from 1836 to 1838 led to a celebrated United States Supreme Court decision in 1857; Eliza Winston, who accompanied her vacationing master to the state in 1860 and obtained her freedom there with the help of local abolitionists; and James Thompson, who arrived at Fort Snelling as a slave in 1827 and remained to become the only black member of the St. Paul Old Settlers Association.[6]

The first census in Minnesota recorded after Minnesota

Dred Scott and his wife, Harriet Robinson Scott, played important roles in American legal and civil rights history when they sued for their freedom in Missouri after living for two years at Minnesota's Fort Snelling. They were married by the fort's Indian agent, Lawrence Taliaferro. The U.S. Supreme Court denied their rights in a famous 1857 court case. Dred Scott was freed later that year by his owner.

was officially organized as a territory in 1849, identified 40 free persons of African descent, 30 of whom lived in St. Paul. The community consisted of seven families, having six male heads of households employed as barbers and cooks; 15 other persons lived outside of family groups. Four of the other 10 blacks resided in Washington County, two each at Fort Snelling and Sauk Rapids, and one in what was then called Wabashaw County. A woman, Maria Haynes, was the only black resident recorded in St. Anthony (now Minneapolis). Eleven states were given as places of birth, with Virginia and Kentucky listed most frequently. According to that census, 95.4% of the black adults were literate.[7]

During the 1850s free blacks and fugitive slaves continued to migrate to Minnesota, where they engaged the attention of the territorial legislature. A St. Paul newspaper characterized the early arrivals as industrious and "attentive to their business," but some legislators feared that the Mississippi River was becoming a conduit for those fleeing from the South and that black people would compete for jobs customarily held by unskilled whites. Some legislators were concerned that the arrivals would become paupers and wards of the territory. As early as 1849 persons of African descent were barred from voting in congressional, territorial, county, and precinct elections, and this prohibition was extended to village elections in 1851 and to town meetings in 1853. The following year a bill, modeled on similar legislation in Ohio, would have required the posting of a personal bond of $300 to $500 as a guarantee of good behavior for every person of African descent intent upon becoming a permanent resident. The bill was defeated.[8]

By the time Minnesota accumulated enough people to apply for statehood in 1857, the national issue of slavery and the sociopolitical divisiveness it engendered found a refrain in the debates of the Minnesota constitutional convention. Convened in the summer of 1857, the body soon deadlocked over the issue of nonwhite suffrage, which was strongly advocated by a vocal group of Republicans. Unable to muster sufficient support, the Republicans compromised by restricting suffrage to white males in exchange for Democratic support of a simpler method by which the constitution could be amended.[9]

In 1860 bills were proposed in the Minnesota legislature to grant persons of African descent suffrage, protect persons claimed as fugitive slaves, and prohibit the confinement of fugitives in the jails of the state. These measures failed to pass, and the House of Representatives defeated one that would have prevented the migration of freed persons of African descent and mulattos to Minnesota and required the registration of those individuals

Underground Railroad

The Mississippi River was a conduit for escaped slaves. Although not formally linked to more well established Underground Railroad routes from southern states into Canada, St. Paul played host to at least one documented station where fugitive slaves were passed on to more secure environments. William Taylor, a barber with a shop on Third Street near the post office, used his daily contacts to help slaves wishing to escape. Taylor, his nephew Joseph Farr, and others would meet steamboats arriving at the St. Paul levee and be tipped off by friends that an escaped slave was on board. The St. Paul network would swing into action to hide the escapee, sometimes in the house of William and his wife, Adeline, and arrange a route to safety. At other times, people such as Taylor and Farr assisted slaves fleeing their southern masters, who spent summer vacations in Minnesota.

already in residence. Further attempts to allow nonwhites to vote were reflected in two statewide referendums seeking to amend the constitution that failed in 1865 by 2,513 votes and that in 1867 by 1,298 votes. By 1868, however, attitudes and political loyalties had shifted sufficiently to carry the issue by 9,372 votes. Thus on March 6, 1868, the legislature amended the state constitution by granting the franchise to males of African descent, "civilized" Indians, and mixed bloods over the age of 21. By so doing, Minnesota became one of the few states to enfranchise its citizens of African descent voluntarily—two years before adoption of the 15th

GRAND
MASS MEETING
OF THE
COLORED PEOPLE OF MINNESOTA,
JANUARY 1st, 1869.

COME ONE! COME ALL!

There will be held in the city of St. Paul, on January 1st, 1869, at noon, in Ingersoll's Hall, A GRAND

MASS MEETING OF THE COLORED PEOPLE
Of the whole State, to celebrate the

EMANCIPATION

Of Four Million Slaves, and to express our gratitude for the bestowal of the elective franchise to the Colored People of this State, and to perfect a State Organization of the Sons of Freedom.

Gov. Wm. R. Marshall, Hon. Morton S. Wilkinson,
Dr. J. H. Stewart, Mayor of St. Paul, Lt.-Gov. Thos. H. Armstrong,
Hon. I. Donnelly, Gen. Levi Nutting,
And others, are expected to be present and address the people.
In the evening, after the meeting, there will be served a Splendid SUPPER, tickets to which will be distributed during the afternoon by the Committee.
NO CHARGE FOR ANYTHING.
Friends from abroad come and help us rejoice. Let there be a grand turn out.

MAURICE JERNIGAN, ENASE WALKER,
ROBERT HICKMAN, PHELAN COMBS, Sr.,
THOS. A. JACKSON, JOHN H. MOFFII,
GEO. B. WILLIAMS, HENRY TROTTER,
JOHN A. JACKSON, WM. SINGLETON,
DAVID EDWARDS, ROBERT BANKS,
GEORGE DENNIS, GEO. ANDERSON,
CLIFTON MONROE, ADDISON DRAKE,
EDMOND JAMES, HENRY GILES,
[St. Paul Press.] Committee.

Eighteen men signed this poster-invitation to the African American community of Minnesota in 1869 "to celebrate the emancipation of Four Million Slaves, and to express our gratitude for the bestowal of the elective franchise to the Colored People of this State, and to perfect a State Organization of the Sons of Freedom." Governor William R. Marshall and several other white politicians were scheduled to address the gathering.

Amendment to the United States Constitution permitted them to vote nationally. In 1869 the legislature also abolished segregation in the Minnesota public schools, a practice that had existed in St. Paul for more than 10 years.[10]

The early legislators' fears concerning black migration to the river towns of Minnesota were not unfounded. The state's black population nearly tripled from 259 in 1860 to 759 in 1870. Doubtlessly included in the latter figure were numbers of former slaves who accompanied Minnesota soldiers returning home from the Civil War. It should be noted, too, that although the legislature passed a law in 1858 establishing a state militia from which black citizens were excluded, 104 black men served in Minnesota regiments during the Civil War.[11]

Other blacks reached the state as the result of a severe labor shortage engendered by repeated calls for volunteers during the Civil War. In 1862 the St. Paul and Galena Packet Company sent agents to St. Louis to hire blacks as deck hands. The *St. Paul Daily Press* of May 16, 1863, suggested that as many as 5,000 persons were needed to supply the region with dependable labor. During the same year, Henry H. Sibley, commanding the state forces in the war against the Dakota Indians, asked for and received from St. Louis teamsters, mules, and "contraband" laborers to be employed by the military at Fort Snelling. When the steamboat *Northerner* approached St. Paul on May 5, 1863, laden with the laborers Sibley had requested, it had in tow a crudely constructed raft containing an additional 76 black men, women, and children. The raft and its occupants had been found adrift on the Mississippi near Jefferson, Missouri, where the *Northerner* encountered it and towed it upstream. The people on board the raft were led by Robert Thomas Hickman, a slave preacher. Many of these people settled in St. Paul.[12]

Another large contingent of contrabands reached St. Paul on May 15, 1863, aboard the steamboat *Davenport*.

Numbering 218 in all, this group included about 100 women and children. They had been sent north under the protective custody of Chaplain J. D. White, and they were escorted by Company C of the 37th Iowa Regiment. Both groups were harassed by Irish dock workers. A portion of these people settled near the fort, where they found employment as teamsters and laborers.

Robert Hickman, leader of a group of slaves from Boone County, Missouri, whose handmade raft was towed up the Mississippi to freedom in 1863.

Communities in the Twin Cities

In general, black migrants probably moved to Minnesota for much the same economic reasons European immigrants did: jobs and opportunities in urban areas and an abundance of land to homestead. They also followed many of the same migratory routes as the Europeans, with a significant number of blacks immigrating from Canada. St. Paul quickly developed a vibrant community that was to be the center of black social and cultural activity in the state well into the 20th century. Not until after 1910 was

St. Paulites lined the levee to greet the Northern Line steamboat *Davenport* about 1870. In 1863 the boat had carried a group of some 200 "contraband" runaway slaves north to jobs and freedom.

St. Paul's hegemony slowly eclipsed by the growth of a Minneapolis enclave. Later St. Paul, Minneapolis, and Duluth exerted a strong magnetic pull on black youths in rural areas. As the children of homesteaders began to come of age, they sought the employment opportunities, marital partners, and an expanded social life offered by cities. As a result during the 20th century the state's rural black population remained small with most blacks (about 90%) preferring to live in the urban areas.[13]

It was the early black settlers of St. Anthony who formed the first formal black religious organization in Minnesota. The village of St. Anthony, settled in 1849, was the earliest municipal unit in what later became the city of Minneapolis, with which it was consolidated in 1872. There sometime in 1857 eight families of free blacks from Missouri, Arkansas, and Illinois settled near the Falls of St. Anthony. Because houses were in short supply, they stayed in the basement of the Winslow House, a hotel, and at Fort Snelling until shelters could be erected.[14]

A few blacks, wanting to worship as Methodists, met in the home of Paul Brown on 4th Avenue Southeast in 1860. They continued to meet in various St. Anthony homes until 1863, by which time their numbers had doubtless been augmented by new arrivals. Two years later the combined black population of St. Anthony and Minneapolis totaled 78 persons, 50 of whom lived in St. Anthony. In 1863 some of them formally organized the St. James African Methodist Episcopal (A.M.E.) Church, but not until 1869 was the congregation sufficiently affluent to take possession of a house of worship formerly occupied by a white congregation at 6th Avenue Southeast and 2nd Street.[15]

Meanwhile in St. Paul two black churches—Pilgrim Baptist and St. Mark's Episcopal—were founded before 1870. Pilgrim, led by Robert Hickman, had erected a building in which to worship. Calling themselves "pilgrims," Hickman's little band met as a religious prayer group, first

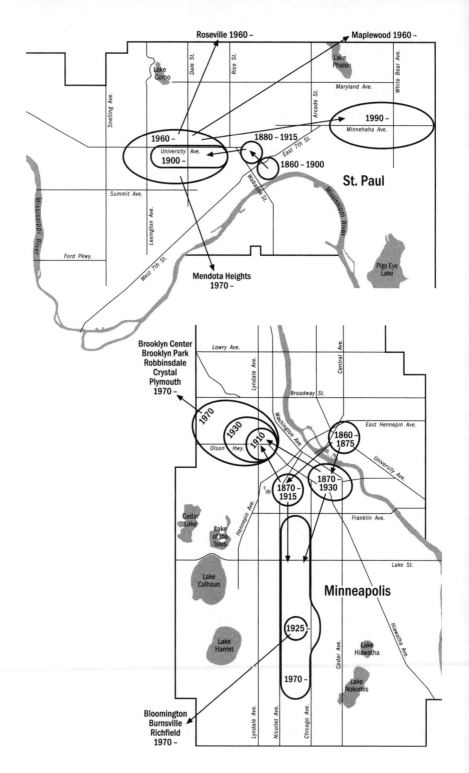

African American Neighborhoods in the Twin Cities, 1860–1990

in the home of Caroline Nelson on 5th Street and then in other residences until November 1863, when they succeeded in renting the lodge room of the Good Templars, a temperance society that met in Concert Hall on 3rd Street. Unable to incorporate as a formal congregation without an ordained minister, and wanting closer bonds with the existing white Baptist community, the congregation authorized Hickman and Thomas Scott to seek mission status from the First Baptist Church of St. Paul in January 1864, which they received.

Between 1864 and 1866 the black parishioners continued to worship separately under Hickman's direction. Lacking resources, they successfully petitioned the trustees of the First Baptist Church in 1866 to intercede and purchase in trust for them a lot located at 12th and Cedar Streets upon which they wanted to construct a house of worship. On November 15, 1866, the Pilgrim Baptist Church was formally organized. Its first structure was completed by February 1871. It was reassembled from the dismantled old Baptist Church in St. Anthony. In 1877 Hickman was ordained, and three years later he at last became the congregation's official pastor.[16]

St. Mark's Episcopal was organized in 1867 and disbanded about 1870 or 1871. Three other St. Paul religious groups came into existence before 1895; one was Methodist, a second was Catholic, and the third was Episcopal. St. James A.M.E. Church of St. Paul, which may have existed as a prayer group as early as 1870, disbanded about 1876, reorganized in 1878, and was able to purchase a permanent home in 1881. St. Peter Claver Catholic Church began in an unstructured way in 1889. With the help of Archbishop John Ireland, a new building was erected for the segregated congregation at Aurora and Farrington Avenues in 1892. St. Philip's Episcopal (mission) Church was an outgrowth of black parishioners attending the Church of the Good Shepherd petitioning the bishop for formal organization

The first all-Negro choir at St. Peter Claver Church, about 1901

of a separate colored congregation in 1894. The congregation initially worshiped in the homes of parishioners until
securing property on the corner of Mackubin and Aurora
Streets in 1905.[17]

From the 1860s until nearly the end of the century,
these churches served a black population distributed
throughout St. Paul, but most heavily concentrated in the
city's commercial district along lower Jackson Street and

along West 3rd, 4th, and 5th Streets between Jackson and Franklin (a block west of Washington). As late as May 1866, a local newspaper complained of a health hazard existing in the "old rookery" on Wabasha Street. The sanitary inspector found the building "inhabited solely by negroes ... of all ages, sexes and shades. In one room thirteen persons were sleeping every night." A month later a group of whites attacked the "negro rookery," destroying the meager personal possessions of the black people living there. In October white neighbors forced the removal of a black family living on West 7th Street because of an alleged outbreak of smallpox among them.[18]

Initial settlement in St. Paul had developed on a bend in the Mississippi River, where the lower levee was located. Into this basin during the early years poured immigrants of ethnically diverse backgrounds—Irish, Germans, Norwegians, Swedes, Jews, and blacks—creating a potpourri of merging ethnic boundaries and residential life. Although there was no discernible pattern of residential segregation, enclaves existed. Locked into a rigid socioeconomic class structure, black people were generally unable to procure employment above low wage levels. Although many male and female heads of households owned substantial amounts of real and personal property by 1870, they were forced to reside in the commercial district where employment existed nearby and rents were generally cheaper. A majority of St. Paul black families lived in single dwellings; a few occupied multiple-family units with white and black neighbors.[19]

In 1870 St. Paul had a total population of 20,030; by 1905 it had become a major urban center with 197,023 people, 28.8% of whom were foreign born. As members of various ethnic groups began to ascend the socioeconomic ladder, they abandoned the commercial district for residential areas on the bluffs, where they re-established enclaves. This movement was accelerated by the extension of horsecar trolley lines in the 1880s and electric streetcars in the 1890s. Among the last groups to leave the commercial district were blacks, who remained there until after the turn of the century.[20]

The physical growth of the black neighborhood was limited by other ethnic residential areas that grew up around the city's commercial core. To the west, where blacks were not welcome, Germans expanded along 7th Street. To the east and below Dayton's Bluff, upper-class white Protestants and French and Irish Catholics developed a fashionable Lowertown neighborhood by the 1870s. To the northeast lived Germans, Swedes, and a few Norwegians. Discrimination and racial antagonism being what they were, the only direction for black expansion lay along the immediate north and northwest corridors leading to residential areas on the western plateau. There the path of least resistance lay through the Jewish community.

During the early 1880s German Jews, who had arrived in St. Paul in the 1850s, began to leave the neighborhood from 8th to 14th Streets for more fashionable homes on Dayton and Summit Avenues. They were replaced by more recent Russian-Jewish immigrants and blacks. By 1900 the pressures of population, coupled with the greater commercialization of the core city, forced blacks farther north and west onto the plateau along Rondo and adjacent streets from Rice to Lexington. Rondo, St. Anthony, Central, Carroll, and University Avenues east of Dale Street became principal centers of black residential life. The movement out of downtown was almost completed by World War I; by 1930 the Rondo area was 47.8% black.

Between 1870 and 1890 the black community had grown over sixfold. The greatest increase occurred among young males from the upper South, attracted in part by expanding employment opportunities. This in-migration added to the imbalance between the sexes; by 1910, 60.5% (1,904 out of 3,144) were black males, a demographic characteristic similar to that of other northern urban centers, which was reflected in such indexes of stability as employment characteristics, marital status, homeownership, and institutional development.[21]

Although black males could be found in a range of occupations by 1910, the majority were unskilled workers employed as porters and waiters. Their largest St. Paul employer in 1880 was the Metropolitan Hotel. It was eclipsed in 1886 by the newly opened Hotel Ryan, most of whose waiters, porters, and cooks were black. Beginning in 1880 the railroad lines headquartered in St. Paul became major employers.[22]

This unidentified man worked as a postal carrier, pictured here on Holly Avenue in St. Paul around 1890 with two of the neighborhood's children.

Blacks were also represented in the skilled trades. Black stonecutters from Georgia were recruited by the Butler Ryan Construction Company for stone and marble work on the new state capitol building. Among those who worked on the capitol building and remained in the area were Casiville Bullard, Benjamin Stevens, and Ike Suddeth. Bullard was unique in that he was a bricklayer, stone mason, and stone cutter. He was a member of the St. Paul Bricklayer's Union, Local #1. In addition to the state capitol building, Bullard is believed to have worked on the Dale Street shops, the U.S. Post Office, Courthouse and Custom House and possibly the St. Paul Public Library. Charles James (1866–1923) rose to the position of president of the St. Paul Trades and Labor Assembly in 1903. He also served as a member of the executive council of the Minnesota State Federation of Labor and was a member of the general executive board, Boot and Shoe Workers Union. This was

Children and elderly residents of the Crispus Attucks Orphanage and Old Folks Home, located in 1910 at Randolph and Brimhall Streets in St. Paul. Founded in 1906 by the city's Industrial Mission Church, it was supported for 60 years by Twin Cities black congregations.

unusual given that blacks were generally excluded from the trade union movement at this time.[23]

Most of the single men roomed in private homes, boardinghouses, or hotels close to their places of work. Their presence created a highly transient population along lower Cedar, Minnesota, and Robert Streets. Those who worked for the railroads usually lived in the commercial district or later on the plateau to the west. Only 41.9% of the eligible black males in Minnesota were married in 1890. By 1910 the figure had risen to 45% for men and 58% for eligible women living in St. Paul. The low incidence of marriage among males might have been the result of a low wage scale that retarded the establishment of independent households. An 1890 survey revealed more blacks rooming or boarding than residing in their own homes. Nevertheless the *Appeal*, a black newspaper, reported on August 24, 1901, that St. Paul had a larger percentage of black homeowners in 1900 than any other city in the United States. Only 14.1% were unencumbered by a mortgage. Ten years later out of 748 dwelling units occupied by black families, 71.3% were rented.[24]

Early Minneapolis

A similar pattern of neighborhood development near the commercial center is suggested by an examination of the city directories for St. Anthony and Minneapolis. Very little is known of the early black community there, but it seems to have been concentrated in the 1860s on the east side of the Mississippi in St. Anthony. Between 1866 and 1875, especially after the two cities merged in 1872, the business district gradually and partially relocated across the river in Minneapolis, producing a corresponding shift by black people who were dependent upon employment there. Lacking transportation and wanting to be near their work, they gradually centered in Minneapolis Wards 2 and 3 (which became Wards 6 and 8 after consolidation).[25]

By 1870 the combined black population of St. Anthony and Minneapolis had more than doubled in 10 years to a total of 162. Between 1875 and 1885 it increased from 175 to 673 and by 1895 it doubled again. By that time black people resided in every ward in the city, but the majority were still concentrated in the area of Nicollet Avenue and 10th Street. After 1900 the perimeters of the black residential area shifted again. By 1910 blacks were beginning to move into North Side neighborhoods being vacated by Jews. Although the southern wards close to downtown still contained a majority of the city's blacks, new enclaves began to develop, especially near 6th Avenue North. This pattern intensified until a ghetto was clearly definable in 1930.

One neighborhood of blacks developed in the Maple Leaf, Humboldt Heights, and Shingle Creek Additions in the vicinity of 50th and Humboldt Avenue North. This

enclave on the northern fringe of Minneapolis was originally settled by black immigrants from Arkansas, Georgia,
Kansas, Kentucky, Missouri, Texas, Virginia, West Virginia,
and Oklahoma. The earliest house was built by John Henry
and Emiline Barnnan in 1914 from materials salvaged from
demolished buildings. By 1930 this community numbered
about 130 and could boast of a Methodist and a Baptist
church.[26]

Like St. Paul, a serious imbalance existed between the
sexes, but unlike St. Paul, it tended to correct itself as the
Minneapolis community matured. In 1890 there were 164
black males aged 15 and older for every 100 females in the
same age group. By 1910 the ratio had fallen to 146 to 100
in Minneapolis, but St. Paul still had 166 men to 100
women. Only 44% of eligible black Minneapolis males
over the age of 15 were married in 1910. Similar employment and homeownership patterns also existed. Men
worked as porters, waiters, cooks, and janitors in hotels,
restaurants, jobbing houses, and on railroad lines, while
black women worked as personal or domestic servants. By
1910, 75.3% of the dwelling units occupied by black people
in Minneapolis were rented.[27]

As the Minneapolis population increased and the
neighborhoods changed, black churches relocated to meet
the spiritual needs of their congregations. Initially established in Ward 4, St. James A.M.E. Church moved several
times and by 1874 was located at 5th Avenue Southeast and
2nd Street. An African Baptist church existed at various
addresses on Harrison Street, and a Free Will Baptist
church stood on 1st Avenue South (Marquette) at the corner of 7th Street.[28]

In 1881 a schism developed in the St. James A.M.E.
Church because a portion of its congregation wanted to
worship closer to the downtown area, while others pre-
ferred to remain in Southeast Minneapolis. As a result,
those in favor of a downtown site withdrew to establish St.

Bobby Marshall

One of the best all-around sports figures Minnesota ever saw was Bobby Marshall. He made his career in baseball and football, but he also played several other sports, including boxing, track, and basketball. He was a multiple threat on the diamond with his ability to play infield, especially first base, and outfield and even pitch. On the gridiron, his usual position was end, though he was known for his game-winning kicks and his savvy as a quarterback. With his expertise, he booamc sought after as a coach.

Born Robert Wells Marshall in 1880, he grew up in Minneapolis. At Central High School he excelled in both baseball and football, leading his school to a championship season in football in 1900. His prowess drew the attention of the University of Minnesota, which allowed him to play reserve and then varsity in his first year with the football team. In his first two years, the team won the Big Ten championship, in no small part due to Bobby's toughness on defense and his touchdown runs. But the real glory came in 1906 when they not only repeated as Big Ten champs but also beat Amos Alonzo Stagg's University of Chicago team 4 to 2 and were dubbed the champions of the west by sports writers. Bobby kicked the game-winning field goal.

Bobby Marshall posed in his football uniform for the 1905 University of Minnesota yearbook.

After graduating in 1907 with a degree in law, Bobby tried to combine playing football in the fall and baseball in the summer with the practice of law. The combination did not work, and he took a job with the state grain inspector's office, a position that allowed him weekends for games. Over the next thirty years he continued playing semi-pro baseball with the St. Paul Colored Gophers and the Minneapolis Keystones and worked in some football.

Bobby often took his message of "good sportsmanship and clean living" to community centers and churches where he talked to young people. He died in 1958. Few noticed his passing, but in 1991 the University of Minnesota named him to its Athletic Hall of Fame.

Peter's A.M.E. Church, which was officially organized in 1886. By 1890 it was able to erect a new building at a cost of $7,000 capable of seating 450 persons. Three additional congregations were established before 1910. They included Bethesda Baptist, organized in 1889; Zion Baptist Mission, organized in the 1880s, reorganized in 1906, and formed into a full-fledged church in 1910; and St. Thomas Episcopal Mission, organized in 1898. In a larger sense, the churches in Minneapolis and St. Paul functioned as community centers offering a wide range of social and recreational activities. Their buildings were used as public meeting halls where issues of the day were discussed. In neither city, however, did black church leaders assume the commanding positions they occupied in other northern urban centers before 1900.[29]

Leadership and Organizations

In 1870 black community leadership was provided by a small but cohesive group of St. Paul men and women. Later they were augmented by a black professional class recruited to serve the needs of the Twin Cities community. Much of the early leadership elite was composed of mulattoes, who, although small in number compared with the overall black population, exercised considerable influence as a class within the black community. The first generation of leaders responsible for the remarkable institutional growth and diversification of the St. Paul community were for the most part men and women without extended formal schooling. Some derived income from various businesses or from land speculation. Many more were hard-working, unskilled laborers.[30]

An article published in the *St. Paul and Minneapolis Pioneer Press* of December 11, 1887, described 13 black leaders with assets of between $5,000 and $100,000. Among them were Thomas H. Lyles and James K. Hilyard.

Community leader James K. Hilyard worked to establish
the Pioneer Lodge of Ancient Free and Accepted Masons
in St. Paul in 1866 and helped to found the
Western Appeal newspaper.

Lyles arrived in St. Paul in 1874 and went into business as a barber. In 1887 he opened a real-estate agency, and by 1906 he became a mortician and established a funeral parlor, which his wife, Amanda, continued to operate after his death in 1920. Hilyard initially settled in St. Paul in 1856. He left the city to volunteer for military service in Philadelphia during the Civil War, returning to St. Paul in 1866 to open a used-clothing store. He also sold real estate and insurance and served as bandmaster for a popular group of musicians who played in the city and on the riverboats.[31]

Both Hilyard and Lyles were organizers. Lyles was active in numerous Republican political clubs, especially in the 1880s. He is credited with convincing the mayor that St. Paul should hire a black policeman in 1881 and that it should have an all-black fire company in 1885. Hilyard was the prime mover in founding black Masonic lodges in St. Paul and Minneapolis in the 1860s, as well as the short-lived St. Mark's Episcopal congregation. Lyles was a charter member and first president of the Robert Banks Literary Society in 1875, and the first grand master of the African Grand Lodge of Minnesota when it was formed by merging six existing lodges in 1894. The Banks Society, which was perhaps the first flowering of intellectual life in the St. Paul black community, was composed of men and women who met to discuss issues of philosophical and practical importance to the race. A local newspaper placed

The first documented African American policeman in St. Paul was Lewis Thomas, shown here in full uniform with his badge and nightstick around 1881.

its membership at approximately 40 persons in 1875.[32]

Lyles and Hilyard may also have played roles in abortive efforts in 1876 and 1880 to publish a black newspaper in St. Paul. It is certain that they quickly became involved in a third, more successful attempt launched in June 1885, which produced the *Western Appeal*. Frederick Douglass Parker, recently arrived from Washington, D.C., was hired as editor, and the paper appeared until 1886, when a financial crisis forced dissolution of the original partnership. Lyles and Hilyard then stepped in to form the Appeal Publishing Company.[33]

The two men were also instrumental in luring professional people to the city. In the 1880s both St. Paul and Minneapolis lacked trained black doctors, lawyers, dentists, and teachers. In the hope of attracting such people, several businessmen placed an article in the *New York Globe* of November 24, 1883, emphasizing the employment potential, business opportunities, and desirability of living in St. Paul. More directly fruitful, however, were Hilyard's efforts to lure John Quincy Adams, former editor of the *Louisville Bulletin*, to the city in 1886. A year later Adams replaced Parker as editor of the *Western Appeal*. Adams was responsible for the arrival in 1889 of Fredrick L. McGhee, the state's first black criminal lawyer, and may have been influential in attracting Dr. ValDo Turner, one of its earliest black physicians.[34]

The combined efforts of these men as well as those of

concerned citizens of both cities attracted other professionals. In 1889 William R. Morris, a young lawyer from Tennessee, and Dr. Robert S. Brown, a recent graduate of Bennett Medical College in Chicago, settled in Minneapolis. The latter became the first black physician licensed to practice in that city. J. Frank Wheaton, a lawyer who joined the Minneapolis group, became the first black elected to the Minnesota legislature, where he represented the 42nd district in the House of Representatives in 1899. Two other arrivals were Charles W. Scrutchin and William T. Francis. Scrutchin took up residence in 1899 in the northern Minnesota town of Bemidji, where he established a reputation as a criminal lawyer. Francis, who became a well-known attorney in St. Paul before World War I, served as a presidential elector in 1920 and was appointed United States minister to Liberia in 1927.[35]

The presence of a growing professional class and the founding of the *Western Appeal* marked a major watershed in the history of the Twin Cities black community. John Q. Adams's rise to a position of prominence between 1887 and 1920 signaled the advent of a new generation of leadership, and the *Appeal* quickly became the people's paper. It defended the race against malicious propaganda, accorded recognition for individual achievement, and spoke out against proscriptive legislation on the national and state levels, while waging a militant local battle for civil rights. Moreover the *Appeal* was an important advertising medium for black businesses, for it encouraged its subscribers to patronize them. Under Adams's capable editorship, the *Appeal*, which had a national readership by 1900, engendered pride and served as a strong unifying force locally. Through the doors of Adams's spacious house on St. Anthony Avenue in St. Paul passed Booker T. Washington, William E. B. DuBois, William Monroe Trotter, and other prominent black national leaders.[36]

When the *Western Appeal* made its appearance, the black population of Minneapolis and St. Paul had grown to approximately 1,400 persons, almost equally divided between the two cities. St. Paul, the older twin, remained the more progressive. As early as 1869 five black men had served on a jury in the Ramsey County court of common pleas, and 10 years later St. Paul had a black dramatic club that helped black citizens of Stillwater stage a benefit for the relief of Kansas refugees.[37] The influence of Lyles had opened the St. Paul police and fire departments to black men in the 1880s and 1890s. After a city militia was authorized in 1880, a black company known as the Rice Guards was formed. The Minnesota Woman's Christian Temperance Union established a mission among blacks in 1884, an effort in which Amanda Lyles was active and which continued on and off until its demise in 1937.[38]

In the 1880s St. Paul blacks also formed organizations designed to combat local de facto segregation and lend support to court tests of proscriptive legislation in the South. The first of these grew out of a suggestion made by Adams in 1887. Upset over a recent court decision that awarded a visiting black architect, William Hazel, only $25 in damages because the Clarendon Hotel refused to provide lodgings for him, Adams proposed in the pages of the *Appeal* of October 22, 1887, that a state convention of black people be assembled to formulate a plan to protect their civil rights. Representatives from 15 counties gathered in St. Paul in December 1887 and after much deliberation formed the Minnesota Protective and Industrial League.[39]

Two years later, rallying to a call for the formation of a national group to

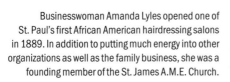

Businesswoman Amanda Lyles opened one of St. Paul's first African American hairdressing salons in 1889. In addition to putting much energy into other organizations as well as the family business, she was a founding member of the St. James A.M.E. Church.

act on behalf of the race, a similar communitywide organization known as the Afro-American League came into
being. Additional leagues were established in Anoka, Duluth, Faribault, Minneapolis, and Stillwater. Adams and
McGhee were sent as delegates to a conference in Chicago
that led to the formation of the National Afro-American
League in 1890, the first national attempt to secure
affirmation of black political and civil rights through judicial process. Still a third group—the Minnesota Citizens
Civil Rights Committee—grew out of league efforts to
raise funds to test the legality of Tennessee's Jim Crow law
in 1891. Undaunted by its lack of success in Tennessee, the
committee went on to raise funds for a second attempt in
Oklahoma.

Adams and McGhee, who served on the national
executive committee, were also undoubtedly responsible
for the fact that the National Afro-American Council's
convention was held in St. Paul in 1902. But McGhee, dis-
illusioned by Booker T. Washington's attempt to dominate
the council's affairs, bolted the organization in 1903 and
closed ranks with W. E. B. DuBois to form the Niagara
Movement two years later. McGhee and Adams again
teamed up, however, to found the Twin City Protective
League, an organization interested in improving living
conditions for blacks in the Twin Cities. In 1912 McGhee
and Dr. Turner were chosen to represent this organization
at the annual conference of the National Association for
the Advancement of Colored People (NAACP) in Chicago.
Their trip helped lay the groundwork for the birth of a St.
Paul chapter of the NAACP in September 1913, a year after
McGhee's untimely death.[40]

In addition to participating in civil rights organizations
that sprang up during the closing decades of the 19th century, black men formed Republican political clubs in the
1880s. As the black electorate grew, its leaders and political
clubs were taken seriously by white Republicans. Although

Fredrick L. McGhee sat for his portrait in Harry Shepherd's studio in 1890, soon after setting up his law practice in St. Paul. Shepherd was a black photographer in St. Paul from 1887 to 1906.

blacks never wielded major political strength at the polls, their votes were assiduously cultivated and in close city elections became the margin of victory. Incumbent officials as well as aspiring candidates accepted invitations to address black audiences at political rallies. Republicans courted these voters, but they rarely delivered lucrative local patronage appointments. Some black leaders were, however, elected as delegates and alternates to national Republican and Democratic conventions. As early as 1888 the *Appeal* sometimes questioned the unswerving allegiance of blacks to the Republican Party, and in the early 1900s independent political clubs were formed that refused to endorse a candidate until his position on race issues was clarified. Such clubs began to wane by 1912, but nationally, blacks continued to support the Republican Party until the ascendancy of Franklin D. Roosevelt.[41]

In spite of the fact that black leaders in St. Paul made impressive strides toward organizational and institutional development between 1870 and 1915, the community lagged far behind other northern urban areas. Blacks did not possess the resources to support their existing organizations and institutions, nor could they bring into being new agencies adequate to serve the community's needs. Discrimination in employment, the failure or inability of blacks to support black businesses, and the indifference of the white community to them prevented the accumulation of surplus capital. For blacks, St. Paul was a working-class community. Social class distinctions as they were known in the East were slow in arriving; the city had no wealthy blacks and no social Brahmins who could claim three generations of free birth. Class differentiation in St. Paul was based upon type of employment rather than upon wealth or breeding.

The Twin Cities from 1910 to 1980

As the years went by, an extended black community was created that included both St. Paul and Minneapolis. Judging by newspapers published in each city, there were few differences between the two by 1910. Although separate social groupings existed, they were closely bound by marriage and family relationships. The number of blacks in both cities was small enough for almost all of the members to be known to each other. Newspapers based in each city circulated freely in the other, and many activities were held jointly.[42]

The genesis of this commonality went back to 1868, when the 30th anniversary of Great Britain's emancipation of West Indian slaves was celebrated in St. Paul on August 1. Attended by black people from St. Anthony and Minneapolis, the event became an annual one, featuring a picnic, commemorative services, and a grand ball. These celebrations continued at least until 1932, frequently attracting visitors from as far away as Duluth. The emancipation of American slaves was also celebrated annually in January, beginning in 1869 after the passage of the Minnesota non-white suffrage law, and a state-wide organization known as the Sons of Freedom came into being the same year. Supposedly composed of all the black men in the state, its purpose was to monitor the general welfare of black residents and provide information on employment, housing, farms for lease, and trade apprenticeships available to them.[43]

After 1915 the initiative and leadership seems to have shifted from St. Paul, and Minneapolis began to replace its older twin as

Dr. O. D. Howard, 1st Sergeant of the Medical Corps of Company A, Minnesota Colored Home Guard, 16th Battalion, with his grandson Raymon Howard Maxell, about 1918. Dr. ValDo Turner was instrumental in establishing this unit of the Home Guard.

Like many Minnesota women, these African Americans made surgical dressings for the Red Cross during World War I. They worked at St. Paul's Welcome Hall, a community center for many activities.

the center of black intellectual, social, and cultural life in the state. The advent of World War I stemmed the flow of European immigrants and created an acute labor shortage in the United States. To meet the demands of a wartime economy, recruiters scoured the South for blacks willing to move to northern industrial centers in return for promises of free transportation, higher wages, and a better standard of living. It is estimated that from 300,000 to 1,000,000 black people left the South in these years, forerunners of an exodus repeated during World War II and the succeeding decades of the 1950s and 1960s.[44]

The Twin Cities were only mildly affected by this massive migration, for the area at that time lacked employment opportunities. The black population of St. Paul grew from 3,144 to 3,376 between 1910 and 1920; Minneapolis registered a hefty increase from 2,592 to 3,927, while Detroit jumped an astounding 611.3% and Cleveland gained 307.8%. The overall growth of the state's black population also remained relatively small—7,084 in 1910 to 8,809 in 1920. By 1920 almost half of the blacks in Minnesota had been born in various southern states.[45]

Many migrants found work on the railroads and in the meat-packing plants. Others took traditional nonunion jobs as redcaps, porters, janitors, waiters, cooks, and barbers. Among those who reached St. Paul between 1912 and 1914 was Clarence Wesley Wigington, an architect who later became the senior architectural designer for the St. Paul City Architect Office.[46]

The influx of southern migrants generated feelings of hostility among members of the black community in both cities. Unfamiliar with urban living and with the subtle

Barbershops still served as gathering places for the black community in the 1950s, when proud father Charles Nichols brought his apprehensive young son Charles, Jr., to Sylvester "Chubby" Young for a haircut at Chubby's Barber Shop at 6th and Lyndale, Minneapolis.

nuances of northern racial detente, they were castigated for their shortcomings by both blacks and whites. Often the black community placed them at the bottom of its social hierarchy.

By 1920 restrictive housing covenants were being used extensively to contain and isolate blacks of both cities. As a result, ghettos emerged. The years between 1920 and 1930 saw a decided shift away from the city centers and a clustering of black people in adjacent neighborhoods. In Minneapolis the near North Side and Seven Corners became the principal ghetto areas. By 1930 they contained 2,100 of the city's 4,176 black people and had the highest incidence of blighted and deteriorating housing, poverty, vice, and crime. A third concentration along South 4th and 5th Avenues between East 35th and 41st Streets was a fairly stable neighborhood of lower-middle-class blacks living in standard housing. The general areas of concentration in Minneapolis did not change greatly during the 1960s and 1970s. Blacks on the near North Side moved west and north from Fremont Avenue to Penn Avenue, while those residing in South Minneapolis moved farther south, nearly to the city limits.[47]

In St. Paul the movement out of the downtown district accelerated after World War I. The concentration along Rondo Avenue and the adjacent avenues between Rice and Dale Streets, constituted a lower-middle-class residential neighborhood of predominantly single-family dwellings. More affluent residents continued to move westward toward Lexington Avenue. The section west of Dale Street (upper Rondo) became known as "Oatmeal Hill," a term indicative of high social standing, while that east of Dale Street (lower Rondo) was called "Cornmeal Valley," a pejorative reference to the growing poverty and greater social dislocation that became apparent in the 1930s. One newspaper in 1926 compared Rondo Avenue to State Street in Chicago and to Lennox Avenue in New York's Harlem be-

The dilapidated housing between the Minnesota State Capitol and downtown St. Paul is shown behind the 1937 Winter Carnival ice palace designed by Clarence "Cap" Wigington, senior architectural designer, city of St. Paul, a prominent African American. The view is from the Capitol looking toward the Cathedral of St. Paul.

cause of the variety of cultural expression it exhibited. In the 1920s it was still relatively free of blighted housing and had a low population density.[48]

Two additional black neighborhoods existed in St. Paul: the West Side Flats and a tenement district in the shadow of the state capitol, where Jews, Italians, and blacks lived in a deteriorating slum. A shanty district along the levee on the west bank of the Mississippi, the flats were inhabited by representatives of 19 ethnic and racial groups, the most notable being Russian Jews, Italians, Irish, blacks, and later Mexicans. All shared a culture of extreme poverty.

While detractors are quick to point out that urban moral ills are directly related to the poverty and illiteracy of delinquent youths under the corrupting influence of criminally minded adults, that does not seem to be the case in Minneapolis. A study of the Minneapolis ghetto conducted in 1923–25 showed that its black residents did not commit major crimes out of proportion to their numbers, as had been alleged. The most frequent arrests were for misdemeanors usually associated with vagrancy, drunkenness, gambling, disorderly conduct, and prostitution.[49]

Nor were the black residents of Twin Cities ghettos illiterate. By 1930 their illiteracy rate was one of the lowest for blacks in the nation, and it was significantly lower than that for foreign-born white, Mexican, and Chinese residents. In Minneapolis only 1.7% of blacks over 10 years of age were illiterate; in St. Paul the figure was 1.2%. (For the country as a whole, the rate was about 16.3%.) By 1970

Young ladies of the Eta Chapter of the Alpha Kappa Alpha sorority at the University of Minnesota, about 1931. Standing (left to right) are Georgia Gray, Alverta Phillips Coram, Pearl Renfro Grissam, Frances Smith Brown, and Henrietta Bonaparte Ridley; seated are Ethel Maxwell Williams, Laverta Huff Diggs, and Victoria Stokers McGlerkin.

census figures for urban areas showed 51.3% of blacks over 25 years old had four or more years of high school, and 66.55% between the ages of 18 and 24 had that much schooling.[50]

The Twin Cities were unusual among northern urban areas in another respect. The wave of racial unrest that swept the nation in the aftermath of World War I did not affect Minneapolis and St. Paul. Although all of the elements of strife were present, black and white leaders, fearing riots like those in Chicago, Detroit, and Omaha, worked to keep the peace.

In this period blacks arriving in the Twin Cities did not have the benefit of community-based agencies to help them secure housing and employment. Usually such assistance was handled by black churches, social clubs, civic organizations, or referrals made by black barbers who obtained information from their patrons. In St. Paul, St. James

Barber and community leader S. Edward Hall was born in Illinois in 1878 and moved to Minnesota in 1900. An active Republican, he operated a barbershop in St. Paul for 62 years and was a founder of the St. Paul Urban League and the Hallie Q. Brown Community Center.

A.M.E. Church in 1915 began publication of the *Helper,* an organ of church news that soon contained job and housing references. The Hall Brothers Barbershop also served as an employment center by posting a list of available jobs, and the Negro Business Leagues of both cities aided in opening new areas of employment.[51]

These combined efforts, however, were not sufficient to process all the new arrivals. As a result, in 1923 the Twin Cities Urban League, a community-wide agency, was founded over the objections of the Chamber of Commerce, whose members felt that such an organization would only encourage further black migration. The joint league functioned until 1938 when separate units were formed for each city.[52]

A second citywide agency came into being in Minneapolis in 1924 when Phyllis Wheatley House opened its doors on October 17 at 808 Bassett Place North in a building that had formerly housed a frame manufacturing plant and Talmud Torah School. W. Gertrude Brown, a graduate of Scotia Women's College, was hired as the first director. The force of her personality quickly made her a leader in the black community. However, her willingness to take strong stands on racial issues often put her in conflict with wealthy white Phyllis Wheatley board members and black male community leaders. In addition to providing recreational activity, the settlement house sponsored baby and dental clinics and classes in black history and culture.[53]

St. Paul had no fewer than three centers, only one of which was not church sponsored. Neighborhood House, located at Indiana and Robertson Streets, had been established in 1897 to serve the West Side Flats. Originally formed as an outgrowth of Mount Zion Temple's efforts to provide assistance for Russian-Jewish immigrants, it was reorganized on a nonsectarian basis in 1903. For years black youths participated in its programs.

In 1916 Zion Presbyterian Church, a black mission

Phyllis Wheatley House founding director W. Gertrude Brown posed with a group of children of varying ages at the Minneapolis settlement house in 1924.

congregation sponsored by several white Presbyterian congregations, opened Welcome Hall Community Center adjacent to the church at the corner of St. Anthony and Farrington Avenues. Under the leadership of the Reverend George W. Camp and his wife, Anna, the center offered recreational activities, Bible classes, a girls' club, and the first day-care facility in the black community.

The Christian Center, founded on February 7, 1926, was the dream of the Reverend Joseph Walter Harris, who wished to provide a nondenominational center for religious education and wholesome recreation. The $40,000

Children gathered for lunch at the Welcome Hall day nursery in St. Paul in 1928.

structure, in 1927 at 603 West Central Avenue, featured classrooms, a library, a music room, social and reading rooms, cafeteria and dining hall, guest rooms, and an apartment for the resident director. Until it burned 10 years later, the center sponsored many social, intellectual, cultural, and religious programs for its patrons.[54]

Two additional facilities were developed in the 1920s as a result of studies conducted by the newly formed Urban League. Convinced of the legitimate need for another community center in St. Paul, the Young Women's Christian Association (YWCA) reorganized its limited "colored" program in 1923 and established a branch at 598 West Central Avenue, which continued to function until 1928. When it closed, the Community Chest empowered the Urban League to organize a new center along racial lines. The result was the Hallie Q. Brown Community Center, which opened under the direction of I. Myrtle Carden in Union Hall at the corner of Aurora and Kent Streets. The

I. Myrtle Carden directed St. Paul's Hallie Q. Brown Community House from 1929 to 1949. Her efforts on behalf of children, working mothers, and senior citizens led to the creation of a variety of social services from home nursing and dental clinics to summer camp programs for children.

structure had originally been built in 1914 by black Masons to house lodge functions and had served as a community meeting hall in earlier years.[55]

Hallie Q. Brown opened only a few months before the 1929 stock-market crash precipitated the Great Depression. By 1931 more than 6,000,000 unemployed workers milled about the streets of the nation's cities looking for work. The Twin Cities were no exception. Black people of Minneapolis and St. Paul had never fully participated in the prosperity of the 1920s. (As early as 1919, it was estimated that the median wage of a black male head of household in the Twin Cities was only $22.55 per week at a time when the United States Bureau of Labor Statistics regarded $43.51 per week as the amount necessary for a family of five.) As the Depression lengthened, Pullman porters, redcaps, and others were laid off by the 11 railroad lines operating out of the Twin Cities. Undercapitalized black businesses were forced to close their doors, and

Employees of the Chicken Shack restaurant, 629 6th Avenue North, Minneapolis, posed for photographer "That Man Smith," about 1930. Owner Tiney Baker Holder stands at the center of the picture.

lawyers and doctors kept creditors at bay only because of their white clients. The sole black group possessing economic security was composed of postal workers employed by the federal government. At a meeting sponsored by the St. Paul Urban League in May 1938, a speaker pointed out that approximately 69% of the city's blacks were either on direct relief or participating in such federal assistance programs as the Civilian Conservation Corps or the Works Progress Administration. Discrimination seems to have been pervasive in the administration of relief, in the placement of persons on government-sponsored projects, and in working conditions.[56]

A mixed group of men attended a Works Progress Administration (WPA) class in printing in St. Paul in 1936.

Minneapolis's Phyllis Wheatley House was the site of this WPA sewing class for women in 1936. Many of the garments they made went to clothe other people in the community.

Two men played checkers near the stove at Itasca County's Thistledew Work Camp, a Civilian Conservation Corps camp, about 1938.

Community leaders gathered around *Spokesman* editor Cecil Newman (front, center) for this 1959 photo in the Spokesman office at 38th St. and 4th Avenue South in Minneapolis to celebrate the 25th anniversary of the newspaper.

The dramatic drop in real income had an adverse effect on community institutions. As church revenues declined, programs were curtailed, ministers were forced onto the relief rolls, and church buildings suffered from lack of maintenance. In spite of economic conditions, however, two black newspapers and one literary magazine were started in Minneapolis. The *Minneapolis Spokesman*, edited by Cecil E. Newman, began publication in 1934 following the failure of his effort to establish a literary magazine called the *Timely Digest* in 1932. The *Spokesman* survived to become the longest-lived black newspaper in Minnesota. Only the *Appeal* had a comparable longevity. The second newspaper, the *Northwest Monitor*, was edited by William Helm. Like Newman's magazine, it failed after only one year.[57]

Not everyone took the events of the Depression passively. Ostensibly angered over the political and economic status of black people in the United States, many of those in the Twin Cities flirted with the Communist Party. In June 1932, 15 black delegates from Minneapolis, Duluth, and St. Paul participated in the Minnesota State Ratification Convention of the Communist Party that nominated Robert Turner, a black worker from St. Paul, as its candidate for the position of Minnesota secretary of state. James W. Ford, the Communist vice-presidential candidate, spoke to an audience at the Hallie Q. Brown Center in September 1932. The party was also active in Minneapolis; in April 1933, Asa Mitchell, a black, was a candidate for fourth-ward alderman on the Communist ticket. But the party's attempt to mobilize black workers met with limited success. They seemed preoccupied by such practical concerns as food, clothing, and jobs rather than by revolt against a political system. Some were more upset by charges of alleged fraternization of black men and white female workers in the party than they were by the diminution of their political rights.[58]

The labor movement offered another avenue by which blacks could collectively express their dissatisfaction. From the late 1920s through the 1930s Frank Boyd was instrumental in organizing a branch of the Brotherhood of Sleeping Car Porters Union in St. Paul. Although fired from his job as a porter for his efforts, the Brotherhood, which was accepted into the American Federation of Labor in 1934, gained collective bargaining rights a year later, resulting in more than $1 million in back payment to porters. In a similar fashion, Nellie Stone Johnson began her long career as a union leader and labor activist in 1934 by spearheading the drive that eventually won union recognition for black workers at the St. Paul Athletic Club.[59]

Even if they could afford them, recreational and entertainment facilities for black people were limited in the

Rondo

In Days of Rondo, *her autobiographical account of coming of age in St. Paul, Evelyn Fairbanks wrote about the social organization of the community and the world of the young black woman of the 1930s and 1940s.*

As important as the Hallie [Q. Brown Community Center] was in our social lives, our families believed that it was important to keep 'our young folks involved' in the churches. While the Hallie developed citizenship as it provided education, entertainment, and physical training, the churches developed a sense of spirituality, stewardship, and service.

My particular service was as a church usher. Teenagers were glad to be active in the churches because it paid the dues for the activities that followed services. Every Sunday, right after church, most of the black teenagers in St. Paul gathered at Fields' drugstore on Rondo and Dale. And we were dressed to kill. When I was sixteen one of my outfits was a gray wool walking suit with a three-quarter-length coat, trimmed from neck to hem with silver fox fur, over a black chiffon long-sleeved blouse. With it I wore a black felt hat with a large gray plume in the back, black patent-leather high-heeled shoes, and a black felt purse, and I carried wrist-length white gloves. I mean, we were dressed to kill. The depression was over and we had jobs that produced money. No more hand-me-downs, mama-made dresses, or look-alike clothes made by WPA workers and distributed by the welfare clothing center.

About once a month, we were joined by our peers from Minneapolis. All of them were as involved with the Phyllis Wheatley House as we were with the Hallie. We had met many times, at games when our teams played each other and at dances at both centers.

It was a strange thing about the two sets of kids. We each reflected the clichés about our hometowns, and therein was the attraction for each other. St. Paul, the seat of old money, produced more conservative people. And the people who worked for them were conservative; and the children of the people

Evelyn, "dressed to kill," stood at the corner of Rondo (left to right) and Dale (top to bottom) in front of Fields' drugstore, about 1945.

who worked for them were conservative. On the other hand, Minneapolis, the home of the nouveau riche, produced a more progressive type of people. And the people who worked for them were more progressive; and the children of the people who worked for them were more progressive.

So the St. Paul boys were fascinated with the flash and style of the Minneapolis girls, who were always ahead of us in fashion and dance steps. The Minneapolis girls returned the favor by thinking that St. Paul boys were honest and trustworthy and some day would make excellent husbands.

We St. Paul girls were taken with the sheer manliness of the Minneapolis boys who, besides being ahead in dance steps and fashion, had a mystery about them. They, in turn, poured their attention on us because we played coy and hard-to-get. (In truth, we weren't any harder to get than our swinging sisters to the west.) Any service that our churches needed was well worth the price to be a member of that 'after-church crowd' at Fields' drugstore on Sunday afternoon to meet those Minneapolis boys.

1930s. None of the major hotels in the Twin Cities allowed them to rent halls for dances or private parties, and none of the better restaurants served them. Much of the entertaining that took place thus necessarily occurred at home or in the Hallie Q. Brown or Phyllis Wheatley Centers. Out of this experience, social clubs evolved that were based on specific recreational interests.

By 1935 more than a dozen fraternal and secret orders and two dozen clubs of various kinds existed in the Twin Cities. Among them were the Credjafawn Social Club (1928), the Aldelphi Club (women's social and civic), Omicron Boule of Sigma Pi Phi Fraternity (1922), the T.S.T.C. Club (1896), and the Sterling Club (1919). With the exception of the Aldelphi Club, these organizations remained

Playing bridge at St. Paul's Hallie Q. Brown Center was the occasion for both sociability and fundraising one evening in 1958.

Members of the
Cameo Club gathered for a Christmas party in the
Fiesta Room at
the Lowry Hotel in
St. Paul in 1950.

active in 2001. The name Credjafawn is an acronym fashioned from the first letters of the names of the charter members. Two years later a junior club for those under the age of 20 was started. As these youths came of age, they were inducted into the senior organization. The club provided the Twin Cities black community with lectures, recitals, and other social, cultural, and recreational affairs. It also started its own credit union and pioneered the first black neighborhood cooperative store in St. Paul.[60]

In 1939 unemployment remained a critical problem in the Twin Cities. Fully 60% of blacks were unemployed compared to 25% of whites. Although the quickening pace of events in Europe would involve that continent in a global conflict before the year ended, no immediate effects were felt by the American economy. Not until 1941, with United States entry into World War II, did wartime mobilization at last end the dreary course of unemployment and Depression. Companies with sizable government contracts began to hire or rehire workers.[61]

Initially the large industries refused to employ black people for war-related work above the level of matrons and janitors. Such a blatantly discriminatory policy, supported by tax dollars and ostensibly sanctioned by the federal government, led A. Phillip Randolph to threaten a march on Washington by 100,000 blacks to protest discrimination in war-contract industries. On June 25, 1941, President Franklin D. Roosevelt issued Executive Order No. 8802 forbidding discrimination in defense industries and setting up a federal regulatory body called the Fair

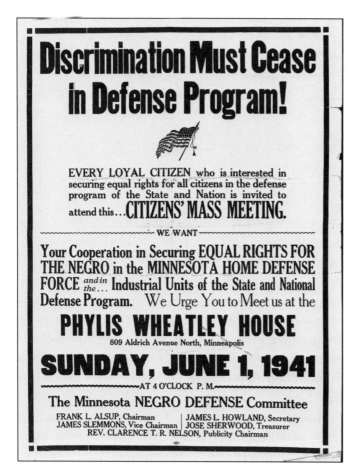

Black Minnesotans were still fighting for equal opportunities, especially in employment, when World War II arrived, and Minneapolis's Phyllis Wheatley House was the site of many meetings.

The *Minneapolis Spokesman* ran a series of cartoons along with articles and editorials supporting the brewery boycott in 1935.

Employment Practice Committee (FEPC) to ensure that the directive was obeyed.

In the Twin Cities some industries and businesses, which had refused to hire black workers before the war and were not recipients of federal contracts, still would not give them jobs. Four of the major breweries—Hamm, Schmidt, Grain Belt, and Gluek—were the targets of a one-year consumer boycott initiated by Cecil Newman and the *Minneapolis Spokesman* in 1935–36. But the companies continued generally to refuse to employ black people throughout and after World War II. Nor were they hired by major department stores in the Twin Cities, except as porters, matrons, elevator operators, or stock clerks, until 1948, when eight large stores took on a total of 14 black salespeople.[62]

A significant breakthrough took place, however, in plants that had never before considered having black workers. More than 1,000 were employed by the Twin City

Ordnance Plant of the Federal Cartridge Corporation at New Brighton. Disavowing the prevailing discriminatory policies of others, the firm assigned blacks at all levels according to their skills, education, and training. At one time this plant employed 20% of the state's adult black population. More than a dozen other firms had favorable records, including the meat-packing industry.[63]

On June 20, 1943, while sitting next to the governor of Michigan during dinner at a national conference of governors, Governor Edward Thye of Minnesota was informed that racial rioting had broken out in Detroit. The Detroit riot was preceded by the Zoot-Suit Riots of Los Angeles, June 4–7, 1943, and followed by the Harlem riot, August 1, 1943. These riots were the result of long-standing racial animosity directed against blacks and Hispanics by whites in large metropolitan areas. Well familiar with the nature of racial discrimination and economic inequality, Governor Thye was concerned that racial intolerance could cause rioting in Minnesota. In December 1943 he assembled leading members of the black and white communities to discuss the condition of Negroes in Minnesota and what was necessary to ensure their well-being. The result was the establishment of the Governor's Interracial Commission of Minnesota. In spring 1945 the commission submitted a report to Governor Thye delineating the employment conditions of Negroes in the state, which was later published as a booklet, The Negro Worker's Progress in Minnesota. An updated report was submitted to Governor Luther W. Youngdahl in 1949.[64]

The employment gains made during the war years were sustained in the postwar period. Additional breakthroughs were achieved in retail sales, public utilities, printing, and manufacturing. Efforts were also made to introduce fair employment practice legislation on the state level, although none passed until 1955. In the area of housing, however, racial discrimination continued unabated. Although restrictive covenants in real-estate transactions were limited by a state law passed in 1937, unwritten agreements often prevented blacks from obtaining houses or inflated their cost far above actual market value. Commercial firms made obtaining home loans and insurance difficult, and the Federal Housing Administration and Veterans Administration often discriminated against black applicants.[65]

In spite of the economic progress made by black Minnesotans during World War II, other problems—notably a shortage of housing—were exacerbated with the return of veterans. The Governor's Interracial Commission found in the mid-1940s that "the overwhelming number" of blacks could not hope to buy or rent outside of definite neighborhoods to which white persons "expect Negroes to be restricted." Urban renewal, Model Cities planning, and freeway construction displaced many residents of these Twin Cities restricted areas in the late 1950s and early

Several black men found work at Harry Schloff's Car Wash and Parking Lot, 143 8th Street in downtown St. Paul, in 1949.

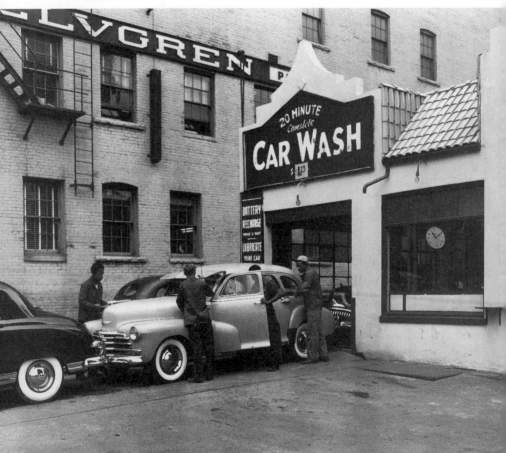

1960s. In their attempts to revitalize the inner cities, urban planners altered socioeconomic and political bases, undermining the stability of neighborhoods, irrevocably damaging certain institutions, and compounding the housing problem.[66]

By 1960 most St. Paul blacks lived in an area that extended west from the central downtown business district, with University Avenue serving as a northern boundary and Selby Avenue being roughly the southern limit. Between 1960 and 1970 there was a slight change in their dispersion in the city because of the dislocations caused by freeway construction and urban renewal. Two additional areas emerged, one along Wheelock Parkway and the other in suburban Maplewood.

Between 1950 and 1970 the black population in Minnesota increased from 13,775 to 34,868, a gain of 153%. Minneapolis experienced a record 436% increase in its black population, while St. Paul registered an impressive 388%. The largest jump occurred between 1960 and 1970, the decade in which the struggle for civil rights reached its greatest intensity in the United States. The majority of these migrants to Minnesota were from the South and from the north-central states.[67]

The reason for this heavy migration to Minnesota is not completely understood. Belief in Minnesota's liberal racial climate, expanded employment opportunities, more generous public assistance, and progressive legislation such as the Fair Employment Practice Act have been credited with influencing some to move to the state. Moreover the Twin Cities had been identified as a training ground for black professional, technical, and managerial people employed by national and international corporations headquartered there. Existing data suggest, however, that the racial climate in the Twin Cities was not qualitatively better than in other northern cities. Moreover employment opportunities for unskilled and undereducated blacks had

Redcaps at the
Union Depot in
St. Paul in 1952

not improved dramatically. During the prosperity of the
1960s, a large number of blacks were absorbed in the service and menial sector of the economy. By 1970 only 18%
were classified as professional, technical, managerial, or
administrative. The median income for black families in
Minneapolis and St. Paul in 1950 was $2,160 and $2,294,
respectively. Although this figure increased to $7,353 and
$7,250 in 1970, almost 67% of black families in both cities
earned less than $10,000 per year in 1970. Approximately
21% were receiving public assistance.

Against this backdrop of discrimination and limited
opportunities, it is not difficult to understand why the
Twin Cities experienced serious civil disorder during the
volatile 1960s. The black population of the two cities was
becoming progressively younger with a median age of 25
in 1960. The average employed black male earned $1,000
less in 1970 than his white counterpart. Unemployment in
St. Paul's Summit-University area in 1965 was estimated at
9.2% for blacks and 6% for whites. In what has been described as a decade of rising expectations, the black urban

Frederick McKinley Jones

One day in December 1912 young Frederick McKinley Jones caught the wrong train out of Chicago. He decided to stay on it and see where it landed him; he arrived in Hallock, Minnesota, in the middle of a blizzard. By spring he found what he wanted—a job overseeing the tractors on the 30,000-acre James J. Hill Farm. Fred Jones, born near Cincinnati, Ohio, in 1892, was a mechanical genius. In his spare time, he built race cars, a snowmobile, and a portable x-ray machine. During service in World War I with the 809th Pioneer Infantry in France, he figured out how to wire the camp for electricity, telephone, and telegraph. After the war, Jones returned to Hallock. Besides building a sound-track movie projector and a machine to take tickets and dispense change, repairing cars and farm machinery, often creating the needed parts, Fred began racing. His record-setting wins with "Number 15" earned him recognition and the nickname "Casey."

The big change came in Fred's life in 1935 and resulted from a truckload of dead chickens. A farmer hauling them to market in summertime ran into disaster when the ice melted, and heat killed his chickens. Fred knew that others had tried to find a way to refrigerate trucks, but the devices shook apart under road conditions. He took the experience he had gained in making race cars handle smoothly, applied the techniques to refrigeration units, placed the units on the top front of the truck, and revolutionized the food industry. Jones and his friend Joe Numero founded Thermo King in Minneapolis to market the product. During World War II, Jones modified the refrigeration methods in order to cool ambulances, field hospitals, and parts of B29s, as well as keep food prepared in field kitchens safe. Over the course of his life, Jones received more than 60 patents, of which 40 were for refrigeration. Jones died in Minneapolis in 1961 at age 68.

Fred Jones at his desk at Thermo King, about 1955

Members of the National Association for the Advancement of Colored People (NAACP) picketed on April 2, 1960, outside Woolworth's in downtown St. Paul to advocate the integration of the store's lunch counter.

population of Minnesota was becoming increasingly resentful of its exclusion from the general prosperity.[68]

The outbreak of civil disorder in the Twin Cities on Labor Day weekend in 1968 was influenced by national events. Upset over intractable unemployment, discrimination in housing, and other forms of discriminatory behaviors, some blacks lost patience with the slow pace towards socioeconomic and political equality. Although the extent of local rioting never reached the levels experienced in Detroit, Newark, the Watts area of Los Angeles, Cleveland, or New York, it produced thousands of dollars in property damage and scores of personal injuries. The civil unrest of the 1960s helped to underscore the disparity in opportunity accorded black Minnesotans.

A poignant example of such disparity was the low number of blacks admitted to the University of Minnesota and the quality of their educational experience. On January 14, 1969, frustrated by the perception of the university administration's lack of support for three demands raised by black students, 60 black students took over the offices of admissions and records in Morrill Hall. The occupation lasted for 24 hours and ended with concessions to the students' demands. The administration's response set in motion several changes that profoundly altered the cultural and academic life of the university, including the establishment of both the Martin Luther King Program and the Afro-American Studies department in 1969. Additionally, the university committed itself to a greater effort to recruit African American students from the Twin Cities and to put in place academic support programs necessary for their retention.[69]

A *Minneapolis Tribune* photographer captured this scene as a truckload of National Guardsmen rode by during racial disturbances in North Minneapolis in July 1967. A television crew also documented the events.

Music Tradition

Music has been a cornerstone of expression for blacks for hundreds of years. In Minnesota it was embodied in lullabies, family group singing, and the church. Many of the songs were spirituals. As the black population grew, the repertoire increased. Churches often had adult, youth, and children's choirs—all performing music for holidays, Sunday services, and other religious occasions.

Groups like the Cantorians, formed in the mid-1950s, combined religious music with popular songs in their performances. Most venues were not open to black musicians so they performed at Hallie Q. Brown and Phyllis Wheatley Community Centers and at social clubs, such as Credjafawn, as well as at the few clubs owned by blacks.

Spirituals, gospel, blues, jazz, rock, and rap all drew on a common experience; some groups emphasized only the religious music of spirituals and gospel, others were more secular.

In the 1960s, Macalester College under-

took an ambitious program to recruit black students and inform others about back culture. Music was part of the program. By 1971 a group of 40 musicians (10 instrumentalists and 30 vocalists) formed an ensemble they named the Sounds of Blackness. From the beginning their mission was to present all forms of African American music, to educate others about its full range, and to instill pride in blacks about their musical heritage. Some recording companies resisted working with a group whose music was so diverse, instead trying to get Sounds to focus on only one type of music. Director Gary Hines and the group held to their mission. By 1988 they teamed up with Jimmy Jam Harris and Terry Lewis and their recording company. Three years later, in 1991, Sounds won the first of two Grammies, this one for their album *The Evolution of Gospel*. The Sounds of Blackness has toured internationally and performed at President Bill Clinton's inaugural.

The Twin City Cantorians performed at a Minnesota Centennial dinner at the Leamington Hotel in Minneapolis in 1958. The dinner was sponsored by Governor Orville Freeman and the Minnesota Centennial Commission in honor of the Scandinavian delegation to the centennial events.

Blacks in Duluth

The city of Duluth, a railroad and shipping center possessing one of the finest deep-water harbors on Lake Superior, developed as the largest city of northern Minnesota in the closing decades of the 19th century after iron ore was found on the nearby Vermilion and Mesabi Iron Ranges. The opening of the Vermilion mines in the 1880s and larger ones on the Mesabi in the 1890s attracted a polyglot group of native-born Americans and immigrants from many nations. Small numbers of blacks were also drawn to the new range communities. John Nichols, an enterprising black man, migrated from Chester, Pennsylvania, to the newly founded mining village of Tower in 1884. For a number of years, he worked as a cook in the Vermilion Hotel there. After it was destroyed by fire, he opened the City Hotel, which he operated until his death in 1907. Nichols derived a handsome income from his business. He married an Irish immigrant woman and raised a family of seven children.[70]

More is known about Duluth's slowly evolving black community. At the time of the city's incorporation in 1857, at least two black men were working as barbers. St. Louis County, in which Duluth is situated, listed 11 black people, seven of whom belonged to the Bonga family. By 1870 there were only 22 blacks in a county population of more than 4,000, and all lived within Duluth's city limits. Thirteen blacks were listed there in 1880, 220 in 1890, and 385 in 1895. The majority in 1886–87 clustered in an area comprising all of the city west of 12th Avenue West and south of 4th Street and including Rices Point, later known as Central Hillside. Unlike St. Paul-Minneapolis, a relatively stable ratio of males (211) to females (205) existed as late as 1930.[71]

It is not known to what extent racial discrimination molded the condition of the community's black residents

during this period. The city's population was characterized by extreme ethnic diversity, and new immigrants continued to arrive in the 20th century. In this structured
environment, black men were relegated to such jobs as
porters, waiters, messengers, janitors, and valets in the
city's hotels, at the Kitchi Gammi Club, or on the railroads.
A few established themselves as independent barbers, and
some opened restaurants during the first decade of the
20th century. At least one person is known to have secured
employment in the police department and another in the
post office before 1910. In short, the patterns discernible in
Duluth are virtual duplicates of those found in the Twin
Cities.[72]

As the Duluth black community continued to grow, institutions arose to meet its needs. In August 1890 the Reverend Richmond Taylor established St. Mark's African
Methodist Episcopal Church on the corner of 4th Street
and 4th Avenue West. A year later its congregation totaled
13 adults and 30 children. Writing in the *Western Appeal* of
August 29, 1891, Pastor Taylor reported with pride the or-

Alexander Miles, a leader in the early Duluth
black community, operated a barbershop
and a real estate office in the 1880s and
1890s. His concern for safety on passenger
and freight elevators led to him to develop
and patent in 1887 a device that would auto-
matically close elevator doors.

ganizing of a black Masonic chapter as one of the congregation's accomplishments.[73]

Other black groups in Duluth included Florence L.
Williams Chapter No. 22 of the Eastern Star, the House-
hold of Ruth Lodge No. 3586 of the Grand United Order of
Odd Fellows—both formed in 1896—and a Knights of
Pythias group, which apparently held regular meetings. By
1910 Doric Lodge No. 3 had been added. Most of these
organizations were offshoots of established lodges in the
Twin Cities and often fell under their jurisdiction. Black
citizens of Duluth maintained close ties with those in St.
Paul and Minneapolis, regularly taking part in the annual
West Indies emancipation celebrations and later the yearly

Reverend Alphonse Reff stands at the pulpit of St. Mark's African Methodist Episcopal (A.M.E.) Church in
Duluth in 1975. Built in 1900 and 1913, the church, located at 530 N. 5th Ave. E., was named to the
National Register of Historic Places in 1991.

Union Picnic held in the Twin Cities. Among the political clubs organized in Duluth to deliver votes for Republican candidates were the Federation of Colored Men of St. Louis County, the Colored Political Club of Duluth, and the Colored Men's Morris and McKinley Club.[74]

As early as 1895 Duluth could also boast a black newspaper, the *World*. Originally published by P. O. Gray, it had subscribers across the bay in Superior, Wisconsin, as well as in Minneapolis and St. Paul. In May 1896 the main office of the *World* was moved to Minneapolis, leaving a branch in Duluth. Nominally independent in its political posture, the paper competed with the *Appeal* and editorially criticized Adams's leadership in community affairs. A second newspaper, the *Progressive News Review*, was initiated and published monthly by Henry Williams after his arrival in Duluth in 1904. Williams also taught violin and was the only black to direct the Duluth municipal band and a children's orchestra.[75]

Despite the flurry of organizational activity, the city's black population did not grow after 1895, remaining at about 400 persons from 1910 to 1930. During the early 1920s the United States Steel Corporation recruited unskilled black laborers from Texas, Louisiana, Mississippi, and Georgia for its plant in the company-built suburb of Morgan Park, but few of these workers stayed. Inferior wages, substandard and segregated housing, discrimination, and harsh weather were cited among the reasons for leaving. While white workers were housed in cinderblock homes constructed by the company in Morgan Park, blacks lived either in company barracks or in substandard houses located in Gary. A lifelong resident pointed out that the steel plant was a major employer of blacks into the 1950s. Long-time black residents of the port city, interviewed in 1974–75, emphasized the steel industry's role in bringing them to the community. One described recruitment procedures used by the steelmakers to secure black workers from Texas for the Morgan Park mill. He regarded their importation as an antiunion effort on the company's part.[76]

After World War I race relations in Duluth became progressively worse. Restaurants, hotels, and theaters, which had reluctantly served blacks before the war, refused to do so or attempted to establish segregated seating. Growing racial antipathy culminated in violence on June 15, 1920, when three black laborers associated with a traveling circus were lynched for the alleged rape of a white girl on a complaint filed by the girl's escort. A crowd variously estimated at between 1,000 and 10,000 stormed the city jail, seized three of the six accused blacks, and hanged them from a street lamp. The National Guard was dispatched to quell the disturbance, and a grand jury was immediately impaneled to investigate the outrage. Eighteen members of the mob responsible for the lynching were indicted, but only two received jail sentences. Ten black men were arrested, two were indicted, and one was sentenced to Stillwater State Prison for a crime few believed ever took place. The St. Paul and Minneapolis NAACP chapters hired lawyers to defend the accused, and the circumstances surrounding the lynching and the ensuing trial received national publicity. This lynching was the only incident of its kind against blacks in the state's history, and it resulted in the passage of an anti-lynching law by the Minnesota legislature in 1921. Shortly thereafter, blacks in Duluth established a local branch of the NAACP, a step they had opposed before the lynching took place.[77]

The Duluth lynchings have been the source of numerous investigative reports over the past 60 years, including a well-researched book by Michael Fedo and a musical on the same subject produced by Penumbra Theatre in St. Paul. Since 2000, in an effort to reconcile its past relative to the lynchings, the city of Duluth sponsored forums, schools added materials on racial equality to coursework, and a

Nellie Griswold Francis

The lynchings in Duluth in 1920 galvanized Nellie Griswold Francis to action. By the time of the next legislative session, she had drafted language for an anti-lynching law. Nellie put years of political experience to work as she campaigned for the bill's passage. She and her husband, William T. Francis, had been active in the Republican Party and in their church, Pilgrim Baptist. As president of the Everywoman Suffrage Club in St. Paul, she had led the organization's campaign to get votes for women. Within months of the lynchings, the anti-lynching bill was introduced in the Minnesota house on February 25, 1921, by Theodore Christianson, a Republican, who four years later became governor of the state. The bill faced little opposition in the legislature and was signed into law on April 20, 1921.

Nellie Griswold was born in Tennessee in 1874 and moved to St. Paul in 1883. After graduating from high school, she worked in the Northern Pacific railroad office. Following her marriage, she returned to work, this time for West Publishing Company. In 1914 she left the work force to spend her energy fighting for women's right to vote. Hardly had that campaign been successful than she turned her skills to passing the anti-lynching law.

In 1927 William Francis was appointed as minister to Liberia, becoming the first black to receive a diplomatic appointment. His career was cut short by yellow fever, and he died in 1929. Nellie returned to live with her family in Tennessee where she died in 1969.

Nellie Griswold Francis,
about 1920

memorial committee prepared to place a monument to mark the site of the lynchings.[78]

Duluth's black population declined after 1930, hitting a low point in 1940 with only 314 persons. Following World War II, however, more blacks migrated to the northern port, so that by 1960 they numbered 565 with nearly 300 more by 1970. (The white population of Duluth decreased from 106,884 to 100,578 in the same decade.) Their mobility within the city is difficult to assess, because census listings by wards have not been available since 1910. Moves to suburban areas were probably minimal because, as one authority noted, "Duluth has a great deal of open space ... [so that] the suburbanizing trend has been substantially accommodated without the creation of extra-city settlements." Examination of census tract schedules for 1960 and 1970 indicated no substantial shift of the black population; increases in various tracts chiefly reflected the growth in the number of blacks.[79]

It has been suggested that the growth in Duluth's black population since 1950 was spurred when the local airport was placed under the jurisdiction of the Central Air Defense Force of the North American Aerospace Defense Command in May 1951. Along with adding black military and civilian personnel, the air base required construction work, supplies and equipment, and other services that boosted the local economy; federal guidelines concerning discrimination probably helped to increase the employment of blacks.

Many black Duluthians in the 1970s felt that theirs was an aging group and that the younger members of the community were leaving to seek opportunities elsewhere. The 1970 census, however, showed that out of 857 persons, 307 were between the ages of 19 and 44; only 117 were in the over-45 age bracket. Ostensibly at least 50.5% of the population was age 19 or under, but these youthful figures might in part be explained by the presence of military personnel and their dependents, a transient population. Continued patterns of discrimination in employment, housing, and racial hostility in the public school system were cited by black residents as contributing factors to the exodus of young people, who often moved to the Twin Cities. By 2000 Duluth had 1,415 blacks.[80]

The 1970 census suggested a low incidence of unemployment among black adults in Duluth, but they were still relegated to service and marginally skilled jobs. Fully 34% were employed as service workers, 20% as clerical, 9% as laborers, and 14% as machinery operators. Only 16% were classified as professional and managerial, with nearly half being elementary and secondary schoolteachers. In 1969 the average black male over 16 years of age earned $6,357, the average black female only $3,500 yearly.

In the past the strength and vitality of urban black communities was measured by the growth and development of community institutions. Although the black churches in Duluth have remained stable and the fledgling NAACP chapter survived, most of the fraternal societies in the late 1970s were affiliates of Twin Cities organizations, a black press did not exist, and social, cultural, or civic clubs had virtually disappeared—all suggesting a community in decline.

The Rural Folk

Of the 39 black or mulatto citizens of Minnesota Territory in 1850, only nine did not live in Ramsey County. Twenty years later Blue Earth, Dakota, Goodhue, Le Sueur, Rice, and Winona Counties each had more than 15 blacks, with concentrations in Hastings (24), Northfield (19), and Winona (37). By the turn of the century only 10 of the state's 82 established counties listed no black persons. The largest enclaves were in Minneapolis, St. Paul, and Duluth, but significant numbers were also clustered in 14 nonurban counties—Aitkin, Anoka, Blue Earth, Dakota, Dodge, Goodhue, Le Sueur, Olmsted, Otter Tail, Polk, Rice, Steele, Washington, and Winona.[81]

Ten years later 8.7% of Minnesota's black people lived in rural areas, but only 29 farms out of 156,137 were operated by black families. Of these, 16 were owned by the operator, 12 were farmed by tenants, and one was managed. The combined acreage owned by black farmers in 1910 was only 2,362, a decrease of nearly 2,000 acres from 1900. The total value of land, buildings, and farm equipment amounted to $128,910. Between 1910 and 1920 both national and state farm operations increased slightly. In the latter year 33 farms, having a total value of $134,670, were operated by black families.[82]

Among the state's rural nonfarm African Americans in 1919 was Jessie Oden, a cook at a resort in Annandale, Wright County.

The types of agricultural operations varied. Some were truck farms located near large urban centers, others produced various cash crops, and a few were homesteads with subsistence agriculture. Among the rare recorded instances of homesteading by blacks in Minnesota was that of the Hosey Posey Lyght family. Dissatisfied with life in a Pennsylvania mining community, Lyght and his wife, Stella, decided to try their hand at farming in South Dakota. A change of plan took them to Duluth in 1913. From there they traveled by steamer up the North Shore of Lake Superior to a site near Lutsen in Cook County, where with their three children they spent the first winter in a one-room cabin. They supported themselves by hunting, fishing, and subsistence farming, supplemented by the wages Lyght was able to earn as a laborer. In addition to the three children brought from Pennsylvania, 12 more were born on the homestead. Later the family owned Northern Lights Resort on Caribou Lake. Most of its patrons were white tourists, but blacks from the Twin Cities, Duluth, Chicago, and Iowa made annual visits to hunt and fish there. Late in the 1960s John R. Lyght was named deputy sheriff of Cook County, and in 1972 he was elected Minnesota's first black sheriff and one of only about a dozen in the United States.[83]

Nellie Stone Johnson, the labor activist, was born on a farm near Lakeville, Minnesota, December 8, 1905. Her parents migrated to the area in 1904. They farmed 180 acres and operated a dairy. Later they purchased and moved to a farm in Pine County, not too distant from Hinckley. Because of her father's involvement in the dairy cooperative movement, the Nonpartisan League, and the Farmer-Labor Party, at an early age she developed an affinity for activism.[84]

Large numbers of black families attempted to homestead near Fergus Falls in Otter Tail County. Approximately 18 family groups from Kentucky made their way to

that north-central Minnesota region as the result of an unusual series of events. In the summer of 1896 the Grand Army of the Republic held a national encampment on the state fairgrounds in St. Paul. Two real-estate agents distributed promotional materials among black veterans from Kentucky extolling the virtues of Fergus Falls. Representatives of a Greenwood, Kentucky, group visited the city later that year, and about 50 persons arrived in April 1897, intending to settle there. Unable to find suitable homesteads or steady employment, some left at the end of the summer, moving to Aitkin County, Akeley and Nevis in Hubbard County, or to Sioux Falls, South Dakota. According to the census, the black community of Fergus Falls numbered 56 in 1900, declining to 34 in 1910 and only 15 by 1970. Most of the members were employed as laborers, while a few farmed. Two businesses are known to have existed, a hairdressing salon and a shoeshine parlor operated by Frank and Minnie Penick.[85]

The Kentuckians were not, however, the first blacks in Fergus Falls. That distinction belongs to Prince Honeycutt, who had lived there since the close of the Civil War. Having served as camp boy for Captain James Compton

Teacher Mattie Anderson and her students posed for a picture at their one-room rural schoolhouse near Fergus Falls around 1910.

during the conflict, Honeycutt returned home with Compton at the war's end. He became a barber, married a white woman who died in a few years, and much later in life took a black woman as his second wife. His children were known for their musical ability, and some of them became schoolteachers in Otter Tail County.

Initially the 1897 migrants to Fergus Falls attended the Swedish Baptist church, but that proved unrewarding because the services were conducted in Swedish. Some joined the Seventh-Day Adventist congregation and others the Methodist Episcopal church. Not until February 22, 1919, did the blacks organize their own Central Baptist Church. After it was officially incorporated on April 2, 1919, with a membership of 22, it bought Bethania Hall, a building formerly occupied by the Bethania Lutheran congregation at 226 Washington Avenue East. The black Baptists remained active until the mid-1940s; after that services were held infrequently.[86]

The Kentuckians who moved from Fergus Falls to Aitkin County seem to have been joined by 25 additional Greenwood families who were persuaded to homestead in Wealthwood, an undeveloped township laid out by a Mille Lacs County real-estate man in 1899. That effort failed, and many of these people settled in Aitkin the following spring. Although predominantly Baptist, some joined the First Methodist Episcopal Church there. In 1914, however, the black parishioners withdrew under the leadership of C. S. Kathan, a white minister, and in October 1915 they organized a nondenominational mission church with 55 charter members. At first, services were held in the homes of members, but the following year a building was erected and formally dedicated. The congregation continued to meet until 1921 when Calvary Baptist Church was organized. The mission church then disbanded, and its remaining membership merged with that of Calvary.[87]

The Dakota County city of Hastings had a growing

Prince Honeycutt stood in front of his barbershop in Fergus Falls, about 1880.

The Best Investment on Earth, is the Earth

Afro-Americans
OF THE TWIN CITIES!

We own and control a large acreage of land in Pine County, Minnesota, which we are offering for sale at reasonable prices and on attractive terms.

The soil is of rich loam suitable for grains, clover, grasses, root crops, gardening and commercial fruit growing.

All lands offered by us have been selected and are some of the very best.

The prices and terms are made attractive with the view of inducing you to become identified with the development of this district.

A word from you will promptly bring complete information.

THIS IS THE OPPORTUNITY FOR AN INVESTMENT OR A HOME.

CHESTER REALTY COMPANY
1227 METROPOLITAN LIFE BLDG.
MINNEAPOLIS   MINN.

The Chester Realty Company promoted land sales in Pine County to readers of *The Appeal* in 1911.

Flora and Simeon Boggs posed for a photographer as part of their Congregational church's group portrait in 1896. During the Civil War she and her two small children had fled their home in Louisiana to the safety of the Union army, where she met Simeon, who was in a colored regiment from Missouri. After the war they accompanied Gen. A. J. Edgerton, the regiment's commander, back to his home in Mantorville. There they resided until her death in 1903 at about age 60 and his in 1905 at about age 85.

black population at the end of the Civil War. About the turn of the century some members of the community erected an African Methodist church at East 5th and Sibley Streets. In October 1907 the church was burned to the ground, the work of "incendiaries," said the local papers. Whether a hostile act was responsible is impossible to say, but the black population of Hastings dropped sharply between 1905 and 1910. In 1970 there were eight blacks listed in the federal census for the city. Thirty years later numbers had grown significantly to 136 (79 blacks plus 57 of mixed race).[88]

In the 20th century other outstate communities showed decreases in the number of black citizens. Stillwater in Washington County had a population of 56 in 1910, one in 1970, and 85 (48 black and 37 mixed race) in 2000. Redwood Falls (Redwood County), which had 39 blacks in

1905 and one in 1970, had 25 (12 blacks and 13 mixed race) in 2000.[89]

In other areas, however, there have been equally dramatic increases in numbers of blacks. Rochester grew from 27 in 1910, to 186 in 1970 and 3,654 (3,064 blacks and 590 mixed race) in 2000; St. Cloud went from 12 blacks in 1910 to 1724 (1,402 blacks and 322 mixed race) in 2000; Red Wing increased from 20 in 1910 to 272 (213 blacks and 59 mixed race) in 2000; and Moorhead grew from eight to 342 (247 blacks and 95 mixed race) in the same period. In 1970 blacks lived in all but five Minnesota counties. By 2000 blacks could be found in residence in all of Minnesota's 87 counties.

Communities in Transition

The closing decades of the 20th century witnessed a significant growth in Minnesota's African American population. Between 1980 and 2001 it increased by 321% while the total population rose by only 17%. Although the black percentage grew by only 2% with respect to the total population, the distribution has shifted slightly since 1980. In 1980, 87% of the black population lived in the state's 15 largest incorporated urban areas. By 2000 the percentage had declined slightly to 77%. Approximately 86.2% of the African Americans in Minnesota reside in five counties (Hennepin, Ramsey, Anoka, Scott, and Washington), with the largest concentrations in Minneapolis (68,818), St. Paul (33,637), Brooklyn Center (4,110), Brooklyn Park (9,659), Bloomington (2,917), Burnsville (2,452), Richfield (2,289), and Eagan (2,166).[90]

The natural increase in the African American population (births over deaths) could not account for such a dramatic change. Therefore, most of the growth can be attributed to migration from other geographic areas. In the 1990s, the business climate for black entrepreneurs was buoyant. According to a census report for 1997, Minnesota was home to more than 3,740 African American businesses, most of them located in the Twin Cities. This expansion in business, industry, and commerce boosted employment opportunities in both the skilled and unskilled sectors of the economy. At the same time, changes in federal and state policies that restricted public assistance contributed to the migration of individuals who perceived Minnesota's regulations to be more liberal. Equally important was the active recruitment effort undertaken by Minnesota's businesses, industries, and educational institutions to find skilled employees to fill high-level technical and administrative positions.[91]

One aspect of the growth not fully captured by the census data is the recent surge in immigration from Africa. Although not African Americans by census definition, Eritreans, Ethiopians, Somalis, Liberians, Nigerians, Ghanaians, Kenyans, and others have increased the number of people of black African descent in Minnesota. Many of these newcomers have found employment in the service sectors of the economy. Their business, religious, and cultural organizations and institutions have helped to develop a more culturally varied state.

The upsurge in the African American population has create several important issues for that community. The recent migration appears to be bifurcated—a relatively small professional class and a large group of working poor whose skills are marginal with respect to employment opportunities. The former are influential, command family incomes exceeding $75,000 per year, and are usually found in decision-making positions in government, business, and education.[92] The unskilled workers are often transient, younger, single heads of households, and dependent on finding work in the central cities of Minneapolis and St. Paul when job growth is occurring in the suburban areas.

Recent studies of the black population have provided

some troubling statistics. African American children are 25% of the school enrollment in St. Paul and 44% in Minneapolis. Yet Minneapolis black students have only a 28% graduation rate from high school and a dropout rate of 48%.[93] Sixty-two percent of these high school students in the metropolitan area live with only one parent or relative. The number of households under the federal poverty guidelines is also increasing. Although crime and gang-related activity in the Twin Cities is lower than in cities of comparable size, Minnesota leads the nation in arrest and incarceration rates of African American males. Racial profiling, unwarranted stops, and arrest or detention of black males of all ages by the police have become contentious political issues involving the state legislature and metro-area police departments. In stark contrast to these bleak numbers, Minnesota has one of the highest levels of post-secondary education achievement among blacks in the work force.[94]

Many benefits accrued to the Twin Cites by the rise in the black population, particularly in the strengthening of the performing arts. A cultural renaissance in the 1970s created venerable institutions like the Penumbra Theatre, one of the few black repertory companies in the nation. In 2002, its twenty-fifth anniversary, Penumbra paid homage to the Pulitzer prize-winning playwright August Wilson, whose early plays premiered on Penumbra's stage. So important has Penumbra become as a cultural icon for the Twin Cities that its founder and artistic director, Lou Bellamy, has often worked with the Guthrie Theater on joint productions.

The Sounds of Blackness, Prince, Terry Lewis, and James "Jimmy Jam" Harris III, all Grammy award winners, constitute in part what became known as the Minneapolis sound in the 1980s and 1990s. The Twin Cities is also home to the Minneapolis Gospel Workshop where contemporary artists have influenced the national scene for

Penumbra Theatre

The lively arts scene in the Twin Cities gained a significant addition in 1976 with the creation of the Penumbra Theatre Company. Lou Bellamy, the founder and artistic director, grew up in St. Paul and studied theater while in college. His vision was both to have a theater dedicated to portraying the lives and experiences of black Americans and to provide work for black directors and actors. Penumbra, housed at the Hallie Q. Brown— Martin Luther King Community Center in St. Paul, is one of the few professional African American theater companies putting on a full season of plays each season. Its efforts have won it national awards. One accomplishment in which the company takes great pride is in having been the first theater to stage three plays by August Wilson, who went on to win the Pulitzer Prize in drama. Wilson commented on Penumbra, "We are what we imagine ourselves to be and we can only imagine what we know to be possible. The founding of Penumbra Theatre enlarged that possibility. And its corresponding success provokes the community to a higher expectation of itself."

In 1992 Penumbra staged *Shakin' the Mess Outta Misery,* which was based on the playwright Shay Youngblood's memories of growing up in a small town in the South in the 1960s

gospel music. The artistic work of James Ransom and the Pilgrim Baptist Senior Choir, Eddy Robinson and the Minneapolis Gospel Choir, Bobby Joe Champion and the Excelsior Choir, and Robert Leigh Morris of the Leigh Morris Chorale have helped to establish the Twin Cities as a vibrant center for innovative gospel music. The vitality of the black musical tradition served to underscore the continued growth and vitality of black churches in the Twin Cities.

The University of Minnesota Library is repository of the Archie Givens Senior Collection of Black Literature. It is one of the premier collections in the nation of first edition and original literary works of African American writers dating back to Phillis Wheatley's poems, which were first published in 1773.

The closing decades of the 20th century witnessed the unprecedented election and appointments of African Americans to public offices. In 1972 James Griffin became the first black police officer to be appointed deputy chief of police in St. Paul.[95] During the 1990s Bill Wilson and Jerry Blakey of St. Paul and Sharon Sayles Belton and Van White of Minneapolis were elected to the city councils. Sayles Belton went on to become the first female and first black mayor of Minneapolis, serving from 1994 to 2001. Another black woman, Jean Harris was elected mayor of Eden Prairie in 1995 and held that office until her death in December 2001. Blakey made an unsuccessful bid for the mayor of St. Paul in 2001. On July 14, 1992, St. Paul Mayor James Schibel appointed William "Bill" Finney, as the first black chief of the St. Paul police.

Several blacks were appointed to head major school districts in the metropolitan area. Carol Johnson was selected to head the Minneapolis School district in 1997, Patricia Harvey in St. Paul in 1999, and Barbara Pulliam in St. Louis Park in 1997. These appointments followed the brilliant career of Richard Green, the first black superintendent of Minneapolis Public Schools, who was appointed in 1980 and served eight years.

In spite of the successes of the African American community, rapid growth during the 1990s has come at the expense of social and political cohesion. Like other major metropolitan areas, the Twin Cities black communities are

Lawyers and Courtrooms

William Morris, Fredrick McGhee, William T. Francis, and Charles Scrutchin were among the first blacks to practice law in Minnesota. The profession expanded slowly as a viable occupation for blacks. In 1921 Lena O. Smith became the first black woman licensed to practice law in the state; throughout her 40-year career, she specialized in civil rights and discrimination cases.

In the mid-1950s blacks breached another barrier when L. Howard Bennett was named a municipal judge in Minneapolis in 1957 and thus became the first black appointed to the bench in Minnesota. Stephen L. Maxwell went on to achieve another first for blacks—district court judge. He had served only a year as municipal judge in St. Paul before being named to the bench in the Second Judicial District (Ramsey County) in 1968. He retired in 1987, having served 19 years on the bench. In 1980 Pamela Alexander became the first black female prosecutor and later in 1983 the first black female appointed to the Hennepin County Municipal Court.

More firsts followed in the 1990s. Alan C. Page, a former Minnesota Viking football player, was elected to the Minnesota Supreme Court in 1992. William McGee was appointed the first black chief public defender in Hennepin County in 1997. And at the federal level, Michael J. Davis became the first African American federal judge in the state in 1994. Four years later B. Todd Jones became the first black to be named U.S. attorney for Minnesota.

Judge Stephen Maxwell in his courtroom in 1968

beginning to experience, in a more general way, the social dislocation that comes from poverty and the lack of access to educational and employment opportunities. A recent study commissioned by the Hennepin County Board of Commissioners found African American males between the ages of 19 and 29 living in Hennepin County to be at risk by every gauge that measures social welfare.[96]

The challenge that lies before the African Americans in Minnesota for the 21st century is to sustain those quality of life indicators—employment, housing, educational achievement, health care—that relate to a higher standard of living while reducing those that signal an erosion of social cohesion and sense of community. To meet that challenge, African Americans can draw on a rich past and the deep roots they have in Minnesota. Black leaders through their commitment to and experience in business, politics, education, religion, and social organizations have left an enduring legacy to guide the community in the coming decades.

Personal Account:
A Labor Organizer's Story

by Nellie Stone Johnson

Nellie Stone Johnson spent her life campaigning for equal opportunity and equal pay for all workers. Taking an active role and standing up for your beliefs were things she learned from her parents. Nellie was born in Lakeville, Minnesota, December 8, 1905, to a farm family. They later moved to Pine County near Hinckley where they operated a dairy farm.

Her fight for fair employment started when she became a founder and organizer for the Hotel and Restaurant Union, Local 665, in Minneapolis in the 1930s. Those associations led her to become a lifelong member of the NAACP and to join the struggle for legislation banning discrimination in employment. Her political activism brought her into contact with Hubert H. Humphrey, and they, with others, organized the merger of the Farmer Labor Party and the Democratic Party to create the DFL. Nellie became the first black elected to city office in Minneapolis when she won a seat on the library board in 1945. Throughout the 1950s and 1960s she continued the battle for civil rights. In 1963 she opened her own business in Minneapolis, Nellie's Alterations, which she ran for more than 30 years. Nellie died April 2, 2002, in Minneapolis. The following is taken from two interviews.

My parents, I guess, conditioned me well. They were very radical people in their sense. My mother was a very good school teacher. I was thinking the other day about history, the reference to black history and the total scheme of history. My mother used to tell me, "You're reading this about yourself: 'You're lazy, you're no good, you're all of these bad things, void of intelligence.' Learn it for your examination, but the real history is thus and so. . . . " And I think that really kind of conditioned me right off the reel. My dad was very active in everything that came along as progress for the small family-type farmer. . . .

The other thing was that my dad was elected to the school board in Dakota County seventy-four years ago [in 1914], I think it was now. And so I cut my teeth on that. This was a constant activity all the time. Then when we moved up to Pine County, why, he had to do some other things

Nellie Stone Johnson at work in her shop, at that time called Nellie's Shirt & Zipper Shop, in the Lumber Exchange Building, Minneapolis, 1980

rather than the school board, which meant going on the township board. They started a Land o' Lakes Creameries Co-op there at Cloverdale. And later he was an appointee of the Roosevelt administration on the REA (Rural Electrification Administration). So my whole life was wrapped up in one organization after the other and every one of these organizations was doing something for people. Later on, my grandmother was only about sixty-five, sixty-six or something like that, and so the folks put her on the school board in Pine County 'cause nobody in our family had time enough 'cause of all these other organizations.

When I came to the city to go to school I still had a year of high school yet, and so I came down here and I was trying to go to school and work and pay attention to what the political climate was. I was working at the Minneapolis Athletic Club and it was a beautiful spot for me to work with the kind of background that I had, because I didn't take any of the surface stuff for granted, and pretty much I had some training as to the fact that these are the enemies of the real people.

The president of Local 665 for many years was George Naumoff. He was also one of the organizers of it. George also worked at the Minneapolis Athletic Club. He was there as a houseman at one time and then he became the freight elevator operator. I was an elevator operator for the most part and, having the least seniority, was the operator of what they called the service elevator where all employees rode. So between George on the freight elevator and me on the service elevator, we came in contact with every employee in the building. So, to begin with, that was just the ideal spot for two people that were concerned about labor.

I had been invited to attend a meeting . . . to talk about whether we should have a union. Word got around the club and my immediate boss had told all of us that if we attended that meeting, we would be immediately fired. I went anyway. . . .

One day I came in to work after one of those meetings. We always had a round-up, so to speak, where our captain talked to all of the employees just before going on duty, did roll call and so forth. And he looked at me (he called everybody by their last name) and he said, "Allen" (that was my maiden name), he said, "Allen, I understand that you attended that meeting last night." He had already said if you attend the meeting you're fired. He said, "If you join that union you're fired." "Well, " I thought, "I'm over the first hurdle now. He's not firing me because I attended the meeting. He's telling me down the line if I join the Union."

So, from there on, I just kept right on talking union and before we know it, we had enough people to call together. . . .

From then on, by being on this service elevator and George being on the freight, before you know it, we had enough votes for a run-off union vote in the club. It went right from there.

One of my mentors was Frank Boyd. I couldn't find a woman so it was two men out there, Reuben Latz from the Cleaners, Drivers, and Laundry Workers Union Local 183 and Frank Boyd from the Brotherhood of Sleeping Car Porters and these two men were friends. They would go to political meetings and all but tear each other apart and then they'd go out and have coffee together. I said, "Boy, there's so much knowledge in these two people!" So I just almost absorbed every word that they said.

I think up to a point Minneapolis and St. Paul were one community on the basis of what the hard issues were. I think that St. Paul had more of the families that had been here for a long time. But on the other hand, Minneapolis had that hard-hitting political kind of movement that was always going someplace, not necessarily right all the time, but always going someplace.

The Minneapolis Urban League was just getting started about that time [1925] and the prime reason for organization there was employment, jobs. NAACP was trying to handle discriminatory cases and so forth. Both were very young organizations at that time. I joined as quick as I could the NAACP. See, I was practically raised on two papers: the *Minneapolis Tribune* and the *Chicago Defender*. I didn't think there were any other papers in the world, you know, for years. I think my father must have started buying the *Defender* in 1905. He must have had the first copy that came off the press.

The social community was pretty much made up of people that worked in these three areas of jobs: the sleeping car porters, dining car, and post office. The people worked at the various private clubs, like the Minneapolis Athletic Club, Minnesota Club in St. Paul, and so forth. We were the next social rung. They looked kindly upon us and I think basically because we had a pay check coming in every week. And a lot of us were going to school and working, too. I think that had some kind of an impact. During the Great Depression in the black community there was something like sixty-four percent of the black community that was on welfare, I remember that quite well. And when you stop and think today that between sixty-five and eighty percent of the black community is unemployed, what has happened in between there? We haven't progressed too far.

By that time [the 1940s] the NAACP was a little stronger in Minneapolis, too. The first thing I did, I went to the unions to get support. There was some strange things that happened, even in the black community. For instance, when we came through in the forties with the first draft of the Fair Employment Practices Act, I tried to get that through the NAACP, and our legal redress chairman at that time moved to table my motion. My goodness, the NAACP . . . ! But I went over to the Central Labor body and got it through. And then Bob Wishart put it through the Hennepin County CIO council. I went out and did some more organizing for memberships in the NAACP, lifted it off the table, and got it passed [in 1946]. But I went to all of the unions in the state, too. . . . In 1953 the NAACP took over the state effort. There had been a fair employment practices state council before that. I participated on the periphery of it, but leadership was a little different and they weren't doing what they should have done, so the state conference of the NAACP decided to take on this job and we did and we passed it. We spent a year evaluating what went wrong with the years that the old council was there, and by 1955 we got it. I remember the date was April 15, 1955, we got it passed.

Even though I was an A F of L member, I did an awful lot of work behind the scenes for the CIO. I used to leave our meetings at [Local] 665 and go over to Harmon Place to the old CIO hall and run off all of their leaflets for the next day's plant distribution there. They didn't have enough women. I don't know why it should be a woman's job, but we did it anyhow, and we'd run off thousands. I'd go home with so much ink and stuff on me, it was just terrible. But those experiences I wouldn't take anything for, cause we really learned how to organize.

Source: Interviews with Nellie Stone Johnson by Carl Ross as part of the 20th Century Radicalism in Minnesota Project, Nov. 17, 1981, p. 1–3, and Mar. 1, 1988, p. 2, 4, 6, 7, 8, 9, 18, 28, MHS.

For Further Reading

Fairbanks, Evelyn. *The Days of Rondo.* St Paul: Minnesota Historical Society Press, 1990.

Holmquist, June D., ed. *They Chose Minnesota: A Survey of the State's Ethnic Groups.* St. Paul: Minnesota Historical Society Press, 1981.

Nelson, Paul D. *Fredrick L. McGhee: A Life on the Color Line, 1861–1912.* St. Paul Minnesota Historical Society Press, 2002.

Reinhart, Thomas E. "The Minneapolis Black Community, 1863–1926." Unpublished paper, St. John's University, 1970, copy in MHS.

Scott, Walter R., ed. *Minneapolis Negro Profile: Pictorial Resume of the Black Community, Its Achievements, and Its Immediate Goals.* Minneapolis: Scott Publications Co., 1970.

Spangler, Earl. *The Negro in Minnesota.* Minneapolis: T. S. Denison, 1961.

Taylor, David Vassar, with Paul Clifford Larson. *Cap Wigington: An Architectural Legacy in Ice and Stone.* St. Paul: Minnesota Historical Society Press, 2001.

———. "John Adams and the *Western Appeal:* Advocates of the Protest Tradition." Master's thesis, University of Nebraska at Omaha, 1971.

———. "Pilgrim's Progress: Black St. Paul and the Making of an Urban Ghetto." Ph.D. Diss., University of Minnesota, 1977.

Notes

1. William O'Hara, "In the Black," *American Demographics*, Nov. 1989; "The Disparity Among the States in Black College Completion Rates: Minneapolis Is as Good as It Gets," *Journal of Blacks in Higher Education*, Winter 1996/97, p. 14–16; *Ebony*, Feb. 1978.

2. U.S. Census 2000 Brief, Black Population 2000, U.S. Census, August 2001, p. 3.

3. U.S. Census, 2000 Redistricting Data: Minnesota.

4. Philip D. Curtin, *The Atlantic Slave Trade: A Census*, 150–58, 231 (Madison, Wis., 1969).

5. George Bonga, "Letters of George Bonga," and Kenneth W. Porter, "Relations Between Negroes and Indians Within the Present Limits of the United States," *Journal of Negro History*, 12:53, 17:361 (Jan. 1927, July 1932); Porter, "Negroes and the Fur Trade," *Minnesota History*, 15:423, 425 (Dec. 1934); Earl Spangler "The Negro in Minnesota, 1800–1865," in Historical and Scientific Society of Manitoba, *Papers*, 3rd series, 20:15 (1963–64); Warren Upham, *Minnesota Place Names*, 93 (3rd ed. rev., St. Paul, 2001).

6. L[ivia] A[ppel], "Slavery in Minnesota," *Minnesota History*, 5:40–43 (Feb. 1923); Jeffrey A. Hess, *Dred Scott: From Fort Snelling to Freedom*, 2–6 (St. Paul, 1975); Earl Spangler, *The Negro in Minnesota*, 19–21, 29–31 (Minneapolis, 1961); Lea Vander Velde and Sandhya Subramanian, "Mrs. Dred Scott," *Yale Law Review*, 106 (Jan. 1997): 1033–1122.

7. The total number is approximate at best, for the methods used to determine race were imprecise, especially for people of mixed parentage. The category "mulatto," for example, which was listed for 25 persons, was really a catch-all and served merely as an indication of color. See Patricia C. Harpole and Mary D. Nagle, eds., *Minnesota Territorial Census*, 1850, 2, 5, 13, 14, 43–45, 47, 49, 50, 53, 66, 72, 80, 88, 90 (St. Paul, 1972).

8. Gary Libman, "Minnesota and the Struggle for Black Suffrage, 1849–70," p. 13–15, Ph.D. thesis, University of Minnesota, 1972; *Minnesota Pioneer* (St. Paul), Sept. 30, 1852; *St. Paul Daily Minnesotian*, Oct. 2, 1856, July 18, 1857; Minnesota Territory, *House Journal*, 1854, p. 255.

9. William Anderson, *A History of the Constitution of Minnesota*, 99–101 (Minneapolis, 1921); Libman, "Black Suffrage," 16–37.

10. Libman, "Black Suffrage," 37–41, 96, 101, 137, 169; Minnesota, *Laws*, 1868, p. 149; William Gillette, *The Right to Vote: Politics and the Passage of the Fifteenth Amendment*, 26, 145 (Baltimore, 1965). A segregated facility was established in February 1859 with Moses Dixon as teacher. *St. Paul Weekly Pioneer and Democrat*, Nov. 5, 1857; *St. Paul Daily Minnesotian*, Mar. 9, 1859; Minnesota, *Laws*, 1869, p. 7; interview of Edward Nichols by author, July 17, 1974, Minnesota Historical Society (hereafter MHS). Nichols married into the Joseph Farr family who had migrated to St. Paul in the 1850s. See [A. Henmina Poatgieter], "The Story of Afro-Americans in the Story of Minnesota," *Gopher Historian*, 23:10 (Winter 1968–69). The interviews cited in this book were taped as part of the Minnesota

Black History Project, 1974–76, and are in MHS.

11. Spangler, *Negro in Minnesota*, 25, 46–50; Minnesota, *Laws*, 1858, p. 232. For example, Charles Jackson, a 14-year-old former slave from Georgia, was among those who arrived in the state with the returning 2nd Minnesota Regiment. He became a barber in Stillwater, where he lived until his death in 1903; see *Stillwater Daily Gazette*, May 5, 1903, p. 3; interview of Jackson's daughter, Mattie J. Rhodes, by author, June 26, 1974.

12. Here and below, see Spangler, *Negro in Minnesota*, 50–53, for a discussion of various versions of the arrival of the Hickman group; Alfred M. Potekin, "Rev. Robert Thomas Hickman: Preacher, (col'd) rail splitter and Slave liberator," 2, in Works Progress Administration (WPA), Annals of Minnesota, Negroes in Minnesota, MHS.

13. [U.S. Bureau of the Census], *Negro Population in the United States, 1790–1915*, 87–89 (New York, 1968); U.S., *Census, 1920, Population*, 3:518, 523, 524.

14. Marion D. Shutter, ed., *History of Minneapolis, Gateway to the Northwest*, 1: 85, 101, 113 (Chicago and Minneapolis, 1923); *Minneapolis Spokesman*, Sept. 29, 1939, p. 3.

15. Here and below, State of Minnesota, *Census, 1865*, 94; Thomas L. Dynneson, "The Negro Church in Minnesota, 1860–1967," 26, master's thesis, Macalester College, 1968; Spangler, *Negro in Minnesota*, 56. An account of the church's founding by Robert Hickman's grandson, John Hickman, appears in *Minneapolis Spokesman*, Apr. 25, 1958, p. 1, 4.

16. Minnesota Baptist State Convention, *Minutes of the Forty-First Anniversary*, 13 (Minneapolis, 1900); Spangler,

Negro in Minnesota, 52–55; *St. Paul Daily Press*, Nov. 7, 1863; *St. Paul and Minneapolis Pioneer Press*, Dec. 11, 1887; Thomas Scott and R. Hickman to First Baptist Church, Jan. 17, 1864; "Report," Jan. 6, 1865, to members of the First Baptist Church, St. Paul; Records of the Board of Trustees, vol. 13, p. 72, all in First Baptist Church Records, MHS; Norma Sommerdorf, *A Church in Lowertown: The First Baptist Church of Saint Paul*, 40 (St. Paul, 1975), 41; Jon H. Butler, "Communities and Congregations: The Black Church in St. Paul, 1860–1900," *Journal of Negro History*, 56: 119–21 (Apr. 1871).

17. *St. Paul and Minneapolis Pioneer Press*, Dec. 11, 1887; *St. Paul City Directory*, 1869, 242, 1870, 269, 1871, 248; *St. Paul Echo*, Jan. 16, 1926, p. 3; Butler, in *Journal of Negro History*, 121–23; Dynneson, "Negro Church in Minnesota," 29, 39, 42, 45, 49.

18. *St. Paul City Directory, 1866*, 263–75, gives a breakdown by wards of ethnic and racial groups based upon the 1865 state census; these figures, which differ from those in Minnesota, *Census, 1865*, 101, have been used here. See also Spangler, *Negro in Minnesota*, 56, 73; *St. Paul Pioneer*, May 31, June 9, Oct. 7, 1866.

19. Alexander, "Blacks in Minnesota," 22–24; Virginia B. Kunz, *St. Paul: Saga of an American City*, 54–65 (Woodland Hills, Calif., 1977).

20. Here and two paragraphs below, see U.S., *Census, 1870, Population*, 1:16; Minnesota, *Census, 1905*, 38, 171; Kunz, *St. Paul*, 69. Maps compiled from data in the *St. Paul City Directory* on ethnic neighborhoods about 1870 and for blacks in 1896 may be found in David V. Taylor, "Pilgrim's Progress: Black St. Paul and the Making of an Urban Ghetto," 44, 45, 47, Ph.D. thesis, University of Minnesota,

1977. See also *St. Paul Pioneer Press*, Sept. 26, 1875; W. Gunther Plaut, *The Jews in Minnesota: The First Seventy-Five Years*, 157,158 (New York, 1959); Calvin F. Schmid, *Social Saga of Two Cities: An Ecological and Statistical Study of Social Trends in Minneapolis and St. Paul*, 148, 155, 157, 162, 163, 177–82, 184 (Minneapolis, 1937). The *St. Paul Echo*, Sept. 18, 1926, p. 2, described Rondo Street as "a riot of warmth, and color, and feeling, and sound."

21. U.S., *Census*, 1870, *Population*, 1:16; [U.S. Bureau of the Census], *Negro Population*, 156. Abram L. Harris, *The Negro Population in Minneapolis: A Study of Race Relations*, 11 (Minneapolis, [1926?]), contains useful data on states of origin of Minnesota's black population, 1880–1920.

22. [U.S. Bureau of the Census], *Negro Population*, 518; *Western Appeal*, June 27, 1885. In 1880 railroads based there were the Chicago, Minneapolis and Omaha, the Northern Pacific, the St. Paul and Duluth, and the St. Paul, Minneapolis and Manitoba.

23. Debbie Miller, "Collections Offer Clues to History of Stonecutters," *Workday Minnesota*, Jan. 8, 2002; Laura Weber, "Casiville Bullard" forthcoming in *Minnesota History*, Spring 2004; David Riehle, "When Labor Knew a Man Named Charles James," *Union Advocate*, Dec. 22, 1997, p. 9–12.

24. Alexander, "Blacks in Minnesota," 22–24; [U.S. Bureau of the Census], *Negro Population*, 252, 273, 471; *Appeal* (St. Paul-Minneapolis), Aug. 24, 1901, p. 3. From 1885 to 1888, this was the *Western Appeal*, see note 35, below. The author obtained the information by compiling black addresses and occupations given in the *St. Paul City Directory*, *1880*, *1890*, and in the 1895 manuscript state census sched-ules and transcribing that data onto city maps.

25. Here and below, Thomas E. Reinhart, "The Minneapolis Black Community, 1863–1926," 16, unpublished paper, St. John's University, 1970, copy in MHS; U.S., *Census*, 1870, *Population*, 1:10; Minnesota, *Census*, *1885*, 25, *1895*, 95; Schmid, *Social Saga of Two Cities*, 78, 179, 183.

26. Carole Zellie, *The Shingle Creek African-American Community, Minneapolis, Minnesota* (Hennepin County, 2000).

27. [U.S. Bureau of the Census], *Negro Population*, 156, 273, 471, 518.

28. *Minneapolis City Directory*, 1873–74, 25, 28; *1875*, 24, 27; *1878–79*, 28, 30.

29. Dynneson, "Negro Church," 40, 48–51; Butler, in *Journal of Negro History*, 56:124, 133; Reinhart, "Minneapolis Black Community," 12; Taylor, "Pilgrim's Progress," 32–37.

30. Addison R. Fenwick, ed., *Sturdy Sons of Saint Paul*, 93 ([St. Paul?], 1899); *St. Paul City Directory*, *1877–78*, 198; *1880–81*, 388; *1906*, 1155; *Western Appeal*, July 18, 1885, Sept. 8, 22, Oct. 6, 1888; *Appeal*, Sept. 1, 1894, July 31, Sept. 25, Oct. 9, 25, 1897, Mar. 26, 1898, May 24, 1902, p. 3, Sept. 11, 1920, p. 3.

31. [Poatgieter], in *Gopher Historian*, Winter 1968–69, p. 17.

32. [Poagieter], in *Gopher Historian*, Winter, 1968–69, p. 17, 18; Spangler, *Negro in Minnesota*, 71; James S. Griffin, *Blacks in the St. Paul Police and Fire Departments*, 1885–1976, 31 ([St. Paul], 1978). See also *Western Appeal*, Sept. 8, 22, 1888; *Appeal*, Sept. 1, 1894; *St. Paul Daily Dispatch*, Feb. 25, 1875; *Minneapolis Tribune*, Mar. 20, 24, 1875.

33. On Sept. 23, 1876, the *St. Paul Daily Dispatch* announced the commencement of a colored newspaper called the *Western*

Appeal, which was Republican in its politics. Another paper, possibly called the *St. Paul Review*, or *Northwest Review*, edited by E. P. Wade was announced in 1880. See *Minneapolis Tribune*, Feb. 11, 1880. On the beginnings of the second, successful *Appeal* in 1888, see David V. Taylor, "John Adams and the *Western Appeal*: Advocates of the Protest Tradition," 10, 14, master's thesis, University of Nebraska at Omaha, 1971, and "John Quincy Adams, St. Paul Editor and Black Leader," *Minnesota History*, 43:283–96 (Winter 1973). See also *Appeal*, Sept. 24, 1910, p. 4.

34. *Appeal*, Sept. 24, 1910, p. 4, Sept. 11, 1920, p. 2; Taylor, in *Minnesota History*, 43:285–87. On McGhee and Turner, see Fenwick, ed., *Sturdy Sons of Saint Paul*, 95; [Poatgieter], in *Gopher Historian*, Winter, 1968–69, p. 18, 20. *St. Paul City Directory, 1897*, 423, lists Dr. T. S. Cook who apparently preceded Turner by a year. See also *St. Paul City Directory, 1898*, 406, 1342. For Adams's role in recruiting McGhee to St. Paul, see Paul D. Nelson, *Fredrick L. McGhee: A Life on the Color Line, 1861–1912*, 10–12 (St. Paul, 2002).

35. [Poatgieter], in *Gopher Historian*, Winter, 1968–69, p. 19–21; *Minneapolis Spokesman*, May 27, 1949, p. 13.

36. Taylor, in *Minnesota History*, 43:288–90. For a list of leaders in the Twin Cities black community, see Taylor, "Pilgrim's Progress," 89.

37. The movement of blacks primarily out of Mississippi and Louisiana into Missouri, Kansas, and Nebraska in 1879 reflected the dissatisfaction of blacks with their social, economic, and political status in the post-Reconstruction South. Encouraged by rumors of available land and freedom for personal pursuits, they left in large numbers only to find themselves without resources and more destitute. For a personal account of the plight of the "exodusters" and the relief effort mounted to alleviate their suffering, see Leslie H. Fishel, Jr., and Benjamin Quarles, *The Black American: A Documentary History*, 189–93 (Glenview, Ill., 1970).

38. U.S., *Census, 1880, Population*, 687, 696; [Poatgieter], in *Gopher Historian*, Winter 1968–69, p. 18; Minnesota Adjutant General, *Annual Report, 1880*, 4 (St. Peter, 1881); Griffin, *Blacks in the St. Paul Police and Fire Departments*, 31; *Minneapolis Daily Tribune*, Mar. 25, 1869, Dec. 4, 1881; *Stillwater Gazette*, May 7, 1879; Bessie L. Scovell, *A Brief History of the Minnesota Woman's Christian Temperance Union . . . 1877 to 1939*, 211 (Minneapolis, 1939).

39. Here and below, see *Western Appeal*, Dec. 24, 1887; Taylor, in *Minnesota History*, 43:291–95; Spangler, *Negro in Minnesota*, 78. The name of the National Afro-American League was changed in 1898.

40. *Appeal*, Oct. 19, 1901, p. 3, Sept. 13, 1913, p. 3; Taylor, in *Minnesota History*, 43:294–26. On the NAACP, see its *Fourth Annual Report*, 1913, p. 57, *Sixth Annual Report*, 1916, p. 20 (New York, 1913, 1916); *St. Paul Dispatch*, Nov. 27, 1969, p. 1. By 1916 the St. Paul chapter had 135 members; Nelson, *Fredrick L. McGhee*, 157–67.

41. *Minneapolis Tribune*, June 15, 1880; *Western Appeal*, Sept. 8, 22, 1888. In the city elections of 1876, Major John Becht was elected Ramsey County sheriff with a plurality of 186 votes, exactly the number of registered black voters turned out by T. H. Lyles in that election. Fenwick, ed., *Sturdy Sons of Saint Paul*, 93. In 1892 McGhee was nominated as a presidential elector of the Republican Party. Later he was an alternate delegate to the Democratic National Convention at Kansas City. He is believed

to have been the first black in the state to be so elected by Democrats. *Svenska Amerikanska Posten*, Sept. 20, 1892; *Appeal*, June 23, 1900, p. 3. See also Spangler, *Negro in Minnesota*, 81; Taylor, "Pilgrim's Progress," 145, 206–11.

42. Community events in both cities received equal attention in the press. See, for example, *Appeal*, Aug. 14, 1909, p. 3, Jan. 22, 1910, p. 1, 3, July 16, 1910, p. 3. Between 1888 and 1919, 13 newspapers competed with the *Appeal*; each lasted only a short time. They were *Afro American Advance*, 1899; *Afro-Independent*, 1888; *Colored Citizen*, 18??; *Minneapolis Observer*, 1890; *National Advocate*, 1917; *Negro World*, 1892; *Northwestern Vine*, 1902; *Protest*, 1892; *Twin City American*, 1899; *Twin City Star*, 1910; *Twin City Guardian*, 1895; *Voice of the People*, 1888; and *World*, 1895. Daniel P. Mikel, "A History of Negro Newspapers in Minnesota, 1876–1963," 12–14, 52–54, master's thesis, Macalester College, 1962.

43. *St. Paul Daily Press*, Aug. 4, Nov. 13, Dec. 31, 1868; *Minneapolis Daily Tribune*, Dec. 20, 1868, Jan. 4, 1870; Convention of Colored Citizens of the State of Minnesota, *Proceedings . . . in Celebration of the Anniversary of Emancipation*, 8, 29–31 (St. Paul, 1869); *Twin City Herald*, July 30, 1932, p. 2.

44. Schmid, *Social Saga*, 123; Henri, *Black Migration*, 68–70.

45. [U.S. Bureau of the Census], *Negro Population*, 99; U.S., *Census*, 1920, *Population*, 3:60; Harris, *Negro Population of Minneapolis*, 11; Henri, *Black Migration*, 69.

46. Spangler, *Negro in Minnesota*, 67; David V. Taylor with Paul Clifford Larson, *Cap Wigington: Architectural Legacy in Ice and Stone* (St. Paul, 2002). Autobiographical accounts of this period are Gordon Parks, *A Choice of Weapons* (New York,

1965; St. Paul, 1986), Anna A. Hedgeman, *The Trumpet Sounds* (New York, 1964), and Taylor Gordon, *Born To Be* (New York, 1929). On the struggle to admit blacks to labor unions, see *St. Paul Echo*, Feb. 13, 1926, p. 1; *Northwestern Bulletin* (St. Paul-Minneapolis), Apr. 22, 1922, p. 2; *Minneapolis Spokesman*, Jan. 12, p. 2, Jan. 19, p. 1, both 1940.

47. Schmid, *Social Saga*, 180, 185; Brian Storton, "Analysis of Minority Dispersion in Minneapolis and St. Paul," 2, term paper, University of Minnesota, 1973.

48. Here and below, see Schmid, *Social Saga*, 180; *St. Paul Echo*, Sept. 18, 1926, p. 2; "Twin Cities Map," in *Fortune*, Apr. 1936, p. 112–19.

49. Maurine Bole, "A Study of Conflict and Accommodation in Negro-White Relations in the Twin Cities," 81, 82, 83, 86, master's thesis, University of Minnesota, 1932; Spangler, *Negro in Minnesota*, 93.

50. Schmid, *Social Saga*, 176; U.S., *Census*, 1970, *Population*, vol. 1, part 25, p. 235.

51. For a general account of postwar unrest, see Louis E. Lomax, *The Negro Revolt* (New York, 1971). See also *Appeal*, Apr. 7, 1923, [p. 1]; Whitney M. Young, Jr., "History of the St. Paul Urban League," 19, 20, Plan B paper, University of Minnesota, 1947, copy in MHS. Copies of the *Helper*, which later became the *Bulletin*, are in the Eva Neal and Family Papers, MHS.

52. Young, "St. Paul Urban League," 22–25, 31; Spangler, *Negro in Minnesota*, 105.

53. Phyllis Wheatley House, "History," notes and typed manuscripts, in Phyllis Wheatley Settlement House Records, MHS; Michiko Hase, "W. Gertrude Brown's Struggle for Racial Justice: Female Leadership and Community in Black Minneapolis, 1920–1940," Ph.D. dissertation, University of Minnesota, 1994.

54. Plaut, *Jews in Minnesota*, 154; *Neighborhood House, 1897–1947, Welcome Hall: A Community House for Colored People, Testimonial as to Welcome Hall and Welcome Hall Playground*, and *Glimpses of the Christian Center, Inc.*—all four pamphlets in MHS.

55. Alice S. Onqué, "History of the Hallie Q. Brown Community House," 12–34, Plan B paper, University of Minnesota, 1959, copy in MHS.

56. *Twin City Herald*, Feb. 25, 1933, p. 1; Bole, "A Study of Conflict," 111; Harris, *Negro Population of Minneapolis*, 28, 29; *Minneapolis Spokesman*, May 6, 1938, p. 1, 6.

57. L. E. Leipold, *Cecil E. Newman: Newspaper Publisher*, 67, 69, 73 (Minneapolis, 1969); Mikel, "History of Negro Newspapers," 17, 63, 121.

58. *Twin City Herald*, May 21, p. 1, June 25, p. 3, Aug. 27, p. 1, Sept. 10, p. 1—all 1932, and Apr. 15, 1933, p. 1.

59. Arthur McWatt, "Frank Boyd: An Uncompromising Labor Leader," *Workday Minnesota*, Jan. 8, 2002; Jennifer Delton, "Labor, Politics and African American Identity in Minneapolis, 1930–50," *Minnesota History*, 57: 427 (Winter 2001–2002); David Brauer, *Nellie Stone Johnson: The Life of an Activist*, 77–92 (St. Paul: 2000).

60. Credjafawn Club, "Report of the President," [1937?], in Credjafawn Social Club Papers, microfilm, roll 2, MHS; "Successful Co-op in St. Paul," in *Eyes: The Negroes' Own Picture Magazine*, June 1946, p. 13. The first two cooperatives were at 384 North Prior Ave. and 989 Payne Ave.; *St. Paul City Directory*, 1942, 251, 1946, 233. The parent organization of these stores was Co-ops, Inc., of St. Paul, established about 1940; it was through this group that the Credjafawn Club established Neighborhood Store No. 3. Information from Arthur W. Stemberg, secretary of the corporation from 1945 to 1969, Apr. 30, 1978.

61. Here and below, see Governor's Interracial Commission, *The Negro Worker in Minnesota*, 6, 16 ([St. Paul], 1945), and *The Negro and His Home in Minnesota: A Report*, 49 ([St. Paul], 1947); Franklin, *From Slavery to Freedom*, 561; *Code of Federal Regulations Title 3—The President, 1933–43, Compilation*, 957 (Washington, D.C., 1968).

62. Leipold, *Cecil E. Newman*, 92–95; Governor's Interracial Commission, *The Negro Worker's Progress in Minnesota: A Report*, 21, 26 ([St. Paul], 1949); *Minneapolis Spokesman*, May 10, p. 1, July 12, p. 1, 1935, and Feb. 14, p. 1, July 24, p. 2, 1936. One brewery reportedly employed a token black as a result of the boycott.

63. Governor's Interracial Commission, *Negro Worker*, 12–14 (1945); Leipold, *Cecil E. Newman*, 94–100; Spangler, *Negro in Minnesota*, 109. Other plants were Brown and Bigelow, Inc., Griggs, Cooper and Co., International Harvester, Minneapolis Honeywell Regulator Co., Munsingwear, Inc., Northwest Airlines, Northwestern Aeronautical Corp., D. W. Onan and Sons, Raymond Laboratories, Inc., Seeger Refrigerator Co., A. O. Smith Corp., Strutwear Knitting Co., and Superior Metal Products Co.

64. Spangler, *Negro in Minnesota*, 151–53; Minnesota, *Laws*, 1955, p. 802–12. For earlier attempts to obtain FEP legislation, see, for example, Minnesota, *Senate Journal*, 1947, p 363; 1949, p. 94; 1953, p. 231. On housing, see Governor's Interracial Commission, *Negro and His Home*, 41–49; Minnesota, *Laws*, 1937, p. 852.

65. Governor's Interracial Commission, *Negro and His Home*, [3], 18; St. Paul

Urban Coalition, *The 1968 Labor Day Weekend in St. Paul: The Events and Their Causes,* 35–46 (St. Paul, 1969).

66. Here and below, see Storton, "Analysis of Minority Dispersion," 2; Governor's Interracial Commission, *Negro Worker's Progress,* 9, 15–19; U.S., *Census,* 1970, *Population.* vol. 1, part 25, p. 596–99.

67. Here and below, see U.S., *Census,* 1950, *Population,* vol. 2, part 23, p. 64, 143–45, 248; 1970, vol. 1, part 25, p. 68, 81–92, 241, 325–28.

68. Here and below, see U.S., *Census,* 1960, *Population,* vol. 1, part 25, p. 333–35; 1970, vol. 1, part 25, p. 93–96, 321–24, 329–32; St. Paul Urban Coalition, *1968 Labor Day Weekend,* 28–32, 68; *St. Paul Pioneer Press,* Sept. 3, p. 13, Sept. 4, p. 4, 1968; *St. Paul Recorder,* Sept. 5, 1968. p. 8. See also Minnesota, *Legislative Manual, 1977–78,* 143, 146; *Minnesota's Black Community,* 63 (Minneapolis, 1976); Ethel V. Mitchell, ed., *Contributions of Black Women to Minnesota History,* 83 (St. Paul, 1977).

69. Office of the President, University of Minnesota, Morrill Hall Investigating Commission Report, May 7, 1979, University of Minnesota Archives.

70. Interview of Edward Nichols, son of John, by author, July 17, 1974.

71. U.S., *Census,* 1870, *Population,* 1:17; 1890, 1:235; 1930, vol. 3, part 1, p. 1217; *Duluth City Directory, 1886–87,* 36; Minnesota Manuscript Census Schedules, 1857, p. 95, 99, 102, 107, 114, microfilm, roll 5, MHS; Minnesota, *Census, 1885,* 65, *1895,* 126.

72. Interview of Ethel Ray Nance by author, May 25, 1974; Nichols interview.

73. *Appeal,* Feb. 22, 1890. A second black congregation was organized about 1890 by Rev. Frederick Lomack, who moved from Minneapolis to Duluth and established Mount Olivet Baptist Church.

It failed to survive, and more than 20 years elapsed before Calvary Baptist Church was formed about 1913. *Minneapolis City Directory, 1890,* 786; *Duluth City Directory, 1914,* 72.

74. Duluth visitors to Twin Cities events appeared in social columns of the *Appeal.* See, for example, July 28, 1900, p. 3, Aug. 4, 1906, p. 5, Aug. 3, 1907, p. 3. See also *World* (Minneapolis and St. Paul—Duluth and West Superior), Apr. 25, May 30, June 6, 13, July 4, Sept. 12, 1896; *Duluth City Directory, 1910,* 118–20. Union picnics were so called because they were sponsored by all the Twin Cities black congregations with the support of other agencies.

75. *The World,* Apr. 25, May 9, June 6, 1896, May 29, Aug. 28, 1897. On Williams, see *Duluth Sunday News-Tribune,* May 16, 1976, Accent North sec., p. 11; interview of William F. Maupins, Jr., by W. J. Musa Foster, Malik Simba, and Seitu Jones, July 31, 1975; *Duluth City Directory, 1906,* 875, *1925,* 729. The duration of his publication is not known.

76. U.S., *Census,* 1910, *Population,* 2:1010; 1930, vol. 3, part 1, p. 1209; author's interviews of Fred D. and Lillian V. Bell, July 9, 1975, and Charles M. and Geraldine H. Stalling, July 30, 1975; Maupins interview. See also Gus Turbeville, "The Negro Population in Duluth, Minnesota, 1950," *Sociology and Social Research,* 36:231–38 (Mar.–Apr. 1952).

77. Spangler, *Negro in Minnesota,* 100–103; Minnesota, *Laws,* 1921, p. 612. See also Michael W. Fedo, *The Lynchings in Duluth* (St. Paul, 2000). Earlier concern about lynching had led to the establishment in 1898 of the American Law Enforcement League of Minnesota; Taylor, in *Minnesota History,* 43:294. Duluth's black population decreased by 42 between 1920

and 1930 while the total population of the city increased by more than 2,000. U.S., *Census*, 1920, *Population*, 3:518; 1930, vol. 3, part 1, p. 1253.

78. See Fedo, *The Lynchings in Duluth*, and *They Weren't Nothin' but Niggers*, produced and directed by Lou Belamy, artistic director, Penumbra Theater since 1976; *Committees of One: Black Migration and Settlement in Minnesota*, a 30-minute, 16 mm. film produced and directed by Walter Goins with the support of the General Mills Foundation, 1982.

79. Here and below, see U.S., *Census*, 1940, *Population*, vol. 2, part 4, p. 166; 1950, vol. 2. part 23, p. 11; 1960, vol. 1, part 25, p. 103; 1970, vol. 1, part 25, p. 80. The *Duluth City Directory*, 1915–16, 89, listed "election districts" rather than wards. See also Daniel J. Elazar, "Constitutional Change in a Long-Depressed Economy: A Case of the Duluth Civil Community," 10, 15, mimeographed article, [1964?], copy in MHS; Bureau of the Census, *Census Tracts: Duluth-Superior*, 1961, p. 14–17; 1972, p. 1–4; "History of Duluth International Airport," mimeographed summary, copy in MHS. In April 1978, Major John W. Volpel, director of information at the base, gave the black military population as 103 and said there was no minority group data for the 1950 to 1970 period.

80. Here and below, see Bureau of the Census, *Census Tracts: Duluth-Superior*, 1970, p. 5; U.S., *Census*, 1970, *Population*, vol. 1, part 25, p. 81–92, 321–24.

81. Harpole and Nagle, eds., *Territorial Census, 1850*, 2, 5, 13, 14, 80, 88, 90; U.S., *Census*, 1900, *Population*, 1:544. The 10 counties were Benton, Houston, Kittson, Lincoln, Marshall, Mille Lacs, Murray, Todd, Wadena, and Yellow Medicine.

82. [U.S. Bureau of the Census], *Negro Population in the United States*, 588, 607, 656; U.S., *Census*, 1920, *Agriculture*, vol. 6, part 1, p. 19, 487.

83. Interview of Norman P. Lyght by author, June 25, 1974. Another black family, that of George Moses, arrived in Cook County from Chicago before 1920. They homesteaded near Good Harbor Bay and were known locally as fine musicians; information from Lyght, Apr. 6, 1978.

84. Brauer, *Nellie Stone Johnson*, 17–46; Nora Murphy and Mary Murphy-Gnatz, *African American Stories in Minnesota*, 42–51 (St. Paul, 2000).

85. Here and below, see *Fergus Falls Daily Journal*, Sept. 16, 1933, p. 2; Grand Army of the Republic, *Journal of the Thirtieth Encampment... St. Paul, Minnesota*, 3 (Indianapolis, 1896); *Fergus Falls City and Rural Directory*, 1919, 104; U.S., *Census*, 1970, *Population*, vol. 1, part 25, p. 148.

86. WPA, Minnesota, Historical Records Survey: Church Records, Otter Tail County, in MHS. Rev. M. W. Withers, a "missionary Evangelist of the Baptist Church, from Minneapolis," served the church during 1918–25, 1928–29, and 1931–36, but it is not certain whether the congregation ever had a resident pastor.

87. Spangler, *Negro in Minnesota*, 67n; WPA, Church Records.

88. Minnesota, *Census, 1868*, 12; U.S., *Census*, 1870, *Population*, 1:18; 1970, vol. 1, part 25, p. 130–59; Lucille H. Doffing, *Hastings-on-the-Mississippi*, 113 (Hastings and Kilkenny, 1976); *Hastings Gazette*, Nov. 2, 1907, p. 3; *Hastings Democrat*, Oct. 31, 1907, p. 2; U.S. Census, 2000.

89. Here and below, see Minnesota, *Census, 1905*, 71; U.S., *Census*, 1910, *Population*, 3:997–1012; 1970, vol. 1, part 25, p. 130–59, 160–62. On blacks in the Moorhead area, see Earl Lewis, "Pioneers of a

Different Kind," *Red River Valley Historian*, Winter 1978–79, p. 14–16. While Stillwater's population decreased, nearby Bayport had 131 Blacks in 1970. It is possible to speculate that industrial diversification and the growth of outstate educational institutions have been responsible in part for increases in some rural black communities; U.S. Census, 2000.

90. U.S. Census, Population-Minnesota 1980, Table 15, Persons by Race: The State Urban and Rural and Size of Place; U.S. Census, 2000; Profile of General Demographic Characteristic—Minnesota, Table 5, Fifteen Largest Incorporated Cities.

91. U.S. Census, Blacks in 1997 Economic Census; Summary of Minority-Owned Business Enterprises—Company Statistic Series, p. 42 (March 15, 2001); Sam Walker, "Deep North: Minneapolis as the New Black Mecca," *Christian Science Monitor*, Sept. 25, 1997, p.1.

92. "The Black Affluent in the Twin Cities," research conducted by author, Spring/Summer 1993. This was a research project designed to capture significant sociological, historical, educational, and economic data on families identified as having incomes exceeding $75,000 annually. Four hundred families were identified as having incomes over $50,000. Eighty-nine families responded to the written survey, five additional families were interviewed.

93. *African American Men Project: Crossroads—Choosing A New Direction, Final Report*, Hennepin County Office of Planning and Development, Jan. 2002, p.21, 25. Also see *African American Men Project: Crossroads—Choosing A New Direction, Research Compendium*, Hennepin County Office of Planning and Development, Jan. 2002; Minnesota State Depart-

ment of Youth, Families and Learning Data Center, District Enrollments by Gender and Ethnicity, 2001–2002 School Year.

94. "The Health and Well-Being of Youth in Minnesota," Urban Coalition (St. Paul, June 2001); "In the Black," *American Demographics*, Nov. 1989. According to the 1990 census, 21.9 % of whites in Minnesota had a bachelor's degree and 6.2% had a graduate or professional degree. In contrast 17.5% of African Americans held bachelor's degrees and 5.2 % held graduate and professional degrees. Minnesota Minority Populations, Working Paper Prepared by Minnesota Planning, Office of State Demographer, Sept. 1994, table 2 and 4; *African American Men Project, Final Report*, 22.

95. James Griffin with Kwame JC McDonald, *Jimmy Griffin: A Son of Rondo—A Memoir* (St. Paul, 2001).

96. *African American Men Project, Final Report*.

Notes to Sidebars

Underground Railroad, p. 6: Deborah Swanson, "Joseph Farr Remembers the Underground Railroad in St. Paul," *Minnesota History*, 56:125–29 (Fall 2000).

Bobby Marshall, p. 19: Steven Hoffbeck, "Black Baseball in Minnesota," *Minnesota History* forthcoming.

Rondo, p. 44: Evelyn Fairbanks, *The Days of Rondo* (St. Paul: Minnesota Historical Society Press, 1990), 142–45.

Frederick McKinley Jones, p. 53: Virginia Hall Ott and Gloria Swanson, *Man with a Million Ideas: Fred Jones, Genius/Inventor* (Minneapolis: Lerner Publications, 1977); Steven M. Spencer, "Born Handy," *Saturday Evening Post*, May 7, 1948, p. 31, 153–54.

Music Tradition, p. 56: Judy M. Henderson, *African-American Music in Minnesota from Spirituals to Rap* (St. Paul: Minnesota Historical Society Press, 1994); "Sounds of Blackness Interview, at Greenbelt, Castle Ashby, England, Aug. 25, 1991, members.aol.com.

Nellie Griswold Francis, p. 62: Martha Reis and Heidi Bauer, "Nellie Griswold Francis," in *The Privilege for Which We Struggled: Leaders of the Woman Suffrage Movement in Minnesota,* ed. Heidi Bauer (St. Paul: Upper Midwest Women's History Center, 1999), 116–21.

Penumbra Theatre, p. 75: penumbratheatre.org; Russell Smith, "Soul Survivor: For Two Decades, Lou Bellamy's Penumbra Theatre . . . ," *Mpls./St. Paul,* Sept. 1995, p. 66–69, 122–24.

Lawyers and Courtrooms, p. 77: www. senate.gov; *Minneapolis Tribune,* Dec. 20, 1957, p. 1, 7; *Minneapolis Star,* Dec. 20, 1957, p. 13A; Barbara Stuhler and Gretchen Kreuter, eds., *Women of Minnesota: Selected Biographical Essays,* rev. ed. (St. Paul: Minnesota Historical Society Press, 1998), 371–72; interview of Stephen L. Maxwell by David Vassar Taylor, June 14, 1974, MHS; *Minnesota Daily,* Nov. 23, 1998; www.mnd.uscourts.gov.

Index

Page numbers in italic refer to pictures and captions.

Robert Banks Literary Society, 21
Rondo area, 14, 33, 44
Rural life and populations, 9, 64–72

St. Anthony, 4, 9
St. James A.M.E. Church, 18–20, 36
St. Mark's A.M.E. Church, Duluth, *59*
St. Mark's Episcopal Church, 9, 11
St. Paul, early settlement, 8–9; and Min-
    neapolis, 28–29, 44; neighborhoods,
    12–14; population, 13, 25
St. Peter Claver Catholic Church, 11;
    choir, *12*
St. Thomas Episcopal Church, 20
Sayles Belton, Sharon, 76
Scott, Dred and Harriet Robinson, 3, *4*
Scrutchin, Charles W., 23
Shepherd, Harry, photograph by, *27*
Slavery, 2, 3; fugitive slaves, 5, 7–8, *71*
Smith, Lena O., 77
Social organizations and lodges, 21,
    45–46, 59–60
Socioeconomics, affluence, 20–21,
    95n92; class differentiation, 28; cur-
    rent problems, 76–78; migration and
    class, 73; statistics, 1–2, 95n94; re-
    stricted opportunities and, 13
The Sounds of Blackness, 56, 74
Spokesman (newspaper), 42; cartoon, *48*
Sports, 19
Steel industry, 60–61
Stevens, Benjamin, 15
Suddeth, Ike, 15
Suffrage, 5–7

Taylor, Richmond, 58–59
Taylor, William, 6

Thomas, Lewis, *22*
Thompson, James, 3
Thye, Gov. Edward, 49
Trade unions, *see* Labor movements and
    unions
Turner, Dr. ValDo, 22, *23*, 26
Twin Cities Urban League, 36

Underground Railroad, 6
Unions, *see* Labor movements and
    unions
University of Minnesota, *34*, 55
Urbanization, 9

Voting, 5–7

Welcome Hall day nursery, *38*
Western Appeal (newspaper), 16–17, 21,
    22, 24, 28, 89–90n33; advertisement,
    70
West Side Flats, St. Paul, 33, 36
White, J. D., 8
White, Van, 76
Wigington, Clarence Wesley, 31, 33
Williams, Henry, 60
Wilson, August, 74, 75
Wilson, Bill, 76
Winston, Eliza, 3
Winter Carnival palace, *33*
Works Progress Administration (WPA),
    40–41
World (newspaper), 60

Young, Sylvester "Chubby," *31*

Zion Presbyterian Church, 36–37

Picture Credits

Names of the photographers, when known, are in parentheses.

Minnesota Historical Society—cover, page x (William Gardner), 3 (Charles Alfred Zimmerman), 4 (both; *Frank Leslie's Illustrated Newspaper,* June 27, 1857), 6, 8 (both), 12, 15, 16, 19 (University of Minnesota, *The Gopher,* 1905, p. 231), 21, 22 (Edward H. Meier), 23, 24, 25 (Kregel Photo Parlors, St. Paul), 27 (Harry Shepherd), 29 (Haynes of St. Paul), 30, 31, 33 (H. G. Heston), 34 (Anderson & Chickett, St. Paul), 35, 37 (Sweet), 38 (*St. Paul News*), 39, 40 (top, "That Man Smith"; bottom, Works Progress Administration), 41 (top, Works Progress Administration; bottom, Civilian Conservation Corps), 42, 44, 45, 46 (Buzz Brown Photographic Studios, St. Paul), 47, 48 (*Minneapolis Spokesman,* July 12, 1935, p. 1), 50 (*St. Paul Dispatch*), 52 (Kenneth Wright), 53, 54 (*St. Paul Dispatch*), 55 (*Minneapolis Tribune*), 56, 59, 62, 65, 67, 70 (*The Appeal,* Sept. 2, 1911, p. 4), 71, 77, 80 (Elizabeth M. Hall)

Booker T. Washington, *A New Negro for a New Century: An Accurate and Up-to-date Record of the Upward Struggles of the Negro Race* (Chicago: American Publishing House, 1900), 55—page 58

Otter Tail County Historical Society, Fergus Falls—page 69

Private collection—page 75

Acknowledgments

Many thanks go to Pat Maus of the Northeast Minnesota Historical Center for answering questions about the black community of Duluth, to Steven Hoffbeck of Minnesota State University, Moorhead, for sharing his research, and to Ben Petry, Daniel Larmouth, and Rebecca Rubinstein for carrying out much of the picture research. I wish to acknowledge the assistance provided by innumerable persons who over the past 30 years have shared research, stories, and data concerning African Americans in Minnesota. A special debt of gratitude is owed to the senior citizens of both the St. Paul and Minneapolis black communities without whose generous help the facts recorded in this book may have been lost to history. I would like especially to thank Josephine Reed-Taylor, my wife of 25 years, for all of the encouragement she has provided.

Minnesotans can trace their families and their state's heritage to a multitude of ethnic groups. *The People of Minnesota* series tells each group's story in a compact, handsomely illustrated, and accessible paperback. Readers will learn about the group's accomplishments, ethnic organizations, settlement patterns, and occupations. Each book includes a personal story of one person or family, told through a diary, a letter, or an oral history.

In his introduction to the series, Bill Holm reminds us why these stories are as important as ever: "To be ethnic, somehow, is to be human. Neither can we escape it, nor should we want to. You cannot interest yourself in the lives of your neighbors if you don't take sufficient interest in your own."

This series is based on the critically acclaimed book *They Chose Minnesota: A Survey of the State's Ethnic Groups* (Minnesota Historical Society Press). The volumes in *The People of Minnesota* bring each group's story up to date and add dozens of photographs to inform and enhance the telling.

Books in the series include *Irish in Minnesota, Jews in Minnesota, Norwegians in Minnesota,* and *African Americans in Minnesota.*

Bill Holm is the grandson of four Icelandic immigrants to Minneota, Minnesota, where he still lives. He is the author of eight books including *Eccentric Island: Travels Real and Imaginary* and *Coming Home Crazy.* When he is not practicing the piano or on the road circuit-riding for literature, he teaches at Southwest State University in Marshall, Minnesota.

About the Author

David Vassar Taylor, dean of the General College at the University of Minnesota, is a scholar of the African diaspora and author of *Cap Wigington: An Architectural Legacy in Ice and Stone,* published by MHS Press in 2001.